My Big O Journey:

Growing up in Owensboro, Kentucky

SHELLY VAN METER MILLER

Copyright © 2015 SHELLY VAN METER MILLER

Madison, Alabama

All rights reserved. No part of this publication may be reproduced, stored for retrieval or transmitted in any form or by any means, electronic, physical, recording or otherwise, without the prior written permission of the author, Shelly Van Meter Miller.

DISCLAIMER AND/OR LEGAL NOTICES: The information presented here represents the view of the author as of the date of publication. This book is for informational purposes only. While every attempt has been made to verify the information provided in this book, the author does not assume responsibility for errors, inaccuracies, or omissions. Any slights of people or organizations are unintentional. All rights reserved.

Author: Shelly Van Meter Miller (Indie Award Winning Author of Tornado Valley: Huntsville's Havoc)

Editors: Diana Miller and Edwina Musante

ISBN: 1507697708
ISBN-13: 978-1507697702

DEDICATION

To my hometown on its bicentennial birthday

SHELLY VAN METER MILLER

CONTENTS

THE BIG O	1
CHICAGO AND THE BIG O	8
LIVING ON THE EDGE	17
CHILDREN OF THE CORN	21
FLOWER CHILD	27
THE BRIDGES OF DAVIESS COUNTY	34
ANOTHER FACE IN THE CROWD	41
WINNER TAKES ALL	49
IF THE SHOE FITS	61
MICHELLE REMEMBERS	73
GROWING PAINS	79
LET THE GAMES BEGIN	106
A TEEN IN TOWNE SQUARE	110
SLEEP IN PEACE	117
HARD GREEN TOMATOES	122
DRIVE-INS AND DINERS	129
HOME OF THE BRAVE	137
NO PARKING	146
THROWED UP	151
WEDDING CRASHERS	156
AND THAT'S THE WAY IT WAS	164
YOU MIGHT BE FROM OWENSBORO IF…	172

ACKNOWLEDGMENTS

Thank you, Mom and Dad, for childhood memories and stories to tell. Thanks to Randy, my better half, who I've spent half of my life with. Twenty-five years and counting...

1

THE BIG O

What is the story behind the Big O? It depends on who you ask. Shrouded in mystery, the Big O is a lot of things to different people. The Urban Dictionary has a throng of articles describing it, yet the exact meaning remains elusive. O is Oprah's signature, and also a nickname for President Obama. A Big O is used to classify math algorithms or could be the name of a popular Japanese cartoon. The Big O's online attention is no surprise based on myriads of definitions. However, the actual Big O is not a math function or any other kind of function. The original Big O is the city of Owensboro, Kentucky. It's the real deal.

Kentucky is known for pretty horses and fast women, or something like that. Owensboro, in Western Kentucky, is known more for its fast racecars, plus the women are pretty too. The city knows all about fast with NASCAR champions, earning it the title of Kentucky's

#1 Sportstown. Owensboro boys learn to drive by age twelve, whether it's a John Deere tractor, a home-built go-cart, or anything in between, which includes racecars and motorbikes.

There are fast wheels and then there are fast balls. Owensboro has always had a heart for baseball whether it was the 1937 Kitty League team, the Owensboro Oilers, which first played at Miller Field, or the 1958 Babe Ruth League, which represented Owensboro in the World Series in Vancouver, Canada. We are a sports-centered city, and all of Owensboro stands behind its athletes. The distinguished sports award played a role in Owensboro's 2013 All-American City Award, coupled with the fact that we have a festival for everything. Across America, Owensboro is known as the Festival City. Owensboro is my hometown; Owensboro is everyone's hometown.

The awards keep coming. The Big O was once considered the new Tulsa of the oil industry, and is still deemed the Barbeque Capital of the World. Other towns may stake claims to our various awards, but we won't hold that against them. Owensboro has always marched to the beat of its own Bluegrass music.

When visitors see children hanging from concrete trees, take in a free show under the sunset, or wind down a spirited Friday evening at the River Park, they get caught up in our small town's aura. It prompts them to ask, "Why?" as in why Owensboro?

Those of us who were brought up in the Big O know why. It is not any one thing we can put our finger on. We are what all our awards say we are; we are Owensboro. The best way to put it: Owensboro is home. Whatever we do to improve the city, modernize it, or make it more marketable to outsiders, it will always be home to us.

It was once my physical home too. Now as I journey through the streets of town, I find it intriguing to imagine the way Owensboro was…My mind travels back in time, once upon a happy time, when I grew up as a little girl in Owensboro during the seventies. It was our country's peacetime, and to me, it had always been that way. I expected the harmony and understanding to remain for the rest of my life. We won't count the Cold War with the Soviet Union since we practically won that one with the Rocky IV movie, before the Wall came tumbling down. I skipped the Civil Rights turbulence, although Watergate was still a bad word and the thought of a Bay of Pigs gave me bad dreams. Sure, we had crises like Three Mile Island, yellow hostage ribbons, and cyanide-laced Tylenol, but those worries seemed far away and would never reach Owensboro.

Hard times like the Depression and war rations were ancient history to our generation. Instead, a donation Rice Bowl was the table centerpiece for us to drop pennies for the poor during supper. My sister said she wished she could drop her Brussels sprouts in the box too. If we did not clear our plates, the faces of the hungry children in Africa stared back at us from their pictures on the donation boxes. When I picture the velvety wallpaper behind our kitchen table, I can almost taste the Shake-n-Bake pork chops and chow mein served on a dinner plate, which stuck to a vinyl placemat. Many of Owensboro's sights and sounds trigger that seventies sensation, and suddenly, I am there.

During the seventies and early eighties, we were focused on who shot JR, Princess Di's wedding, Michael Jackson's Thriller video, and Cabbage Patch Doll adoption. We did not live in fear, knew our neighbors intimately, never locked doors, and assumed everyone in America was middle class like us.

My family was typical of most in Owensboro. For years, there were four of us children: Michael, Lesley, Tracy, and me, the eldest. Everyone noticed Michael's hair, white as a Q-tip. Both my sisters came into the world with shiny red hair and received even more attention. My baby brother, Van, received the most attention by surprising Mom and Dad in their early forties. Someone always put his boot in his mouth when asking Dad about the fifth addition, "Did you plan this one?"

Instead of pleading the fifth, Dad answered. "He's the only one we planned," as he patted Mom's swollen belly. The expectant father enjoyed giving an unexpected answer which caused jaws to drop. As for me, I had to seek attention in other ways.

My generation grew up in peace and bloomed where we were planted. We roamed freely and drank in life by gulping, especially the water from a garden hose. Despite chewing stray gumballs found on the grocery store floor, and regular meals of Vienna sausages, Cheez Whiz, and potato sticks from a can, we didn't die. If pinching an inch was an issue, a Body Trimmer was attached to a doorknob, a vibrating belt jiggled belly fat, and solar jogging suits reflected throughout town. Fitness was not taken seriously until Olivia Newton John suggested Let's Get Physical and Jane Fonda coerced us with leg warmers and a sweat headband.

Tradition was paramount. I did something a certain way because that was how Mom did it. And she did it that way because of her mom. Sunday visits to Grandmother's house were also a given. Grandmother and her two sisters lived on the same block, three copycat homes side by side. It was Aunt Hazel, Grandmother in the middle, and then Aunt Jo, pronounced "Ain't Jo." Considering the whole package, you couldn't find a tradition deeper than that.

Sundays after church, I swung on Grandmother's backyard hammock, intoxicated with the fresh bread aroma from the bakery I could see across the alley. As the hammock swayed higher, I chanted the commercial, "That's what I said, Bunny Bread." A horde of distant cousins swung on Aunt Jo's swing set in the next yard. With so many cousins, I couldn't remember all of their names. I wandered over every Sunday to reintroduce myself and to see if any donuts were left.

Adult relatives took turns reading the paper at Aunt Jo's kitchen counter, barring the way to the donuts and pimento cheese sandwiches. They could have the pimento cheese. I once got sick on it after riding while facing backwards in our family station wagon. I no longer cared for the sandwich tradition, even if the crusts were pre-peeled. It was hard to eat something after seeing it in reverse order, even Fruit Loops.

Relatives discussed local politics over the glazed donuts with a toothpick dangling from their teeth. It mesmerized me to watch the toothpick wave up and down as they carried on spirited conversations. Next, was Aunt Hazel's house. Aunt Hazel 'greased my palm,' which meant, gave me money to listen to her stories. She even remembered when the Titanic sank.

When we were sick at home, Mom forced us to gargle with warm salt water. We hated it and would rather our throats swell shut. "Why do we have to do this?" we wailed.

"Because Aunt Hazel did this and…"

"Yes, we know. She lived to be 101."

Aunt Hazel was never sick. Therefore, we ate pears mixed with cottage cheese to go with olive and cream cheese sandwiches because Aunt Hazel did. We imitated her eating habits to prevent sickness, while she probably ate certain foods because she liked them. The rest of Sunday was spent in Grandmother's basement, watching The Wonderful World of Disney. After my show, I fell asleep while Dad and Grandmother watched Kojak.

We thrived on traditions, whether it was stock car racing or donuts minus the pimento cheese. We were proud of our hometown but didn't know it until we left for our annual KEA trip to Panama City Beach for spring break. On the drive back from the beach, we nagged, "Are we almost home?" When you were on the way to Owensboro, you were almost home.

And I almost was. From my present Alabama home, I was driving back to my Owensboro hometown, just off the Bluegrass Parkway. After dodging pot holes as large as the sinkhole at the Corvette Museum, I came upon the exit curve with the flashing warning lights and smiled. It was difficult to decrease speed when I was so close to home, and it was always a dilemma which road to take from there. My husband, not an Owensboro native, is usually is in the driver's seat and inevitably asks, "Do I turn here?"

"You can," I say. Someday he'll find that all roads lead to home. No matter where I roam, Owensboro will always be my home. Just like the buffaloes which once roamed Frederica Street, Owensboro is our little home on the range. And I thought it would never change.

2

CHICAGO AND THE BIG O

At my thirty year class reunion, I asked a former classmate if she had any scoop on Owensboro that could go in a book.

"My aunt used to work at the Motor Inn with the Mob," she said.

The Motor Inn, formerly the Hotel Owensboro, was once a southern hotel of distinction. The five story hotel boasted 150 rooms, renting for $3/night in 1926. The inn advertised two of the most marketable luxuries: fireproof quarters with a bathroom in every room. Bob Hope even stayed overnight at the Hotel Owensboro, and once said, "I grew up with six brothers. That's how I learned to dance-waiting for the bathroom." It was possible the luxury bathrooms appealed to gangsters too.

Before the hotel, located on Fourth and Frederica was razed in 1990, I worked in its basement for two whole days as a telemarketer, the glory days of both the cold caller and prank caller. Two days of telephoning the unsuspecting populace was two days too long. I promptly quit and missed the Mob scene, if there was one.

My dad hinted of a Mob story when he said, "I was Bugs Moran's paper boy for a week." I Googled the name and bingo! I was in the middle of Mob mania with my search taking me to the streets of Chicago, "back in the U.S.A., back in the bad old days." I was then curious as to how Dad could have delivered Moran's newspaper.

The events in Chicago happened before my time, but what occurred then in the big city had a bearing on our little city of Owensboro. The ties which linked our two cities before I was born enabled me to see my hometown through different eyes. I will not look at dogwood trees, bathtubs, Cedar Street, or even Valentine's Day the same way again.

Besides both ending in an o, comparing Chicago to Owensboro was like apples and oranges, or in this case, onions. Ever since I could remember, Owensboro had always been the Big O. Although it was the fourth largest city in Kentucky, it could hardly be compared to the likes of Chicago. It was still the Big O to us; we named it and the name stuck. However, we had nothing to do with calling the Windy City of Chicago a skunk or smelly onion like the Indians did. While New York was the Big Apple, "Shikaakwa," a.k.a. Chicago meant smelly onion and was nicknamed the Big Onion. Hence the Big O.

The Big O of Chicago parallels the Big O of Owensboro in several ways. Chicago's Navy Pier juts into Lake Michigan like Owensboro's River Walk borders the waterfront property on the Ohio River. Grant Park's Buckingham Fountain has nothing over Smothers Park's synchronized fountains. Our fountains do not change colors to music, but a shell 'thing' with live music underneath changes to pastel every now and then. And Chicago, where is your waterfall? The Big O's waterfall practically cascades into the Ohio River. So the Hampton Inn would never pass for the Hancock Center and Gabe's Tower was a far cry from the Sears Tower, but the comparisons between the Big O's do not end there.

Coincidentally, the two towns had their 1920's villains in common too. Regardless of how many times I said as a teenager, "Owensboring" was not a word. The wilderness of Owensboro's past was bewildering, not boring. Murder never went out of style, and it certainly was not boring. Like scenes from The Great Gatsby, the Roaring Twenties in both of the Big O's was heightened with jazz music, cigar lounges, big Cadillacs, bootleggers, and illegal gambling. It was remarkable how the paths of both Owensboro and Chicago intertwined. One of those paths crossed in a manicured neighborhood in Owensboro, while another originated in our country backwoods.

Both Owensboro and Chicago were forced to endure the Prohibition years in their own ways when the United States government sought to control alcohol sales in order to control loose morals. Prohibition's result in Chicago: gangsters bootlegged themselves to power and battled deadly turf wars on the streets. Prohibition's result in Owensboro: the economy tanked as local distilleries and farmers were put out of business when both liquor, and the corn which made it, couldn't be marketed.

Drunkenness had always been marketable though. Speakeasy saloons with bogus business names popped up in both cities. These taverns required special passwords to enter and customers were to "speak easy" in the secret bars so police would not suspect the undercover business. The speakeasy bartenders distilled alcohol easier in bathtubs, which was how bathtub gin came to be. Desperate drinkers guzzled from the tub as fruit juices and soda disguised the bathwater flavor. Toda, the cocktail was born. Citizens became more creative in their quest for intoxication.

Owensboro's Glenmore Distillery went against the grain, so to speak, with its 'white lightning' whiskey. The federal government allowed the industry to stay in business to produce alcohol for the country's medicinal purposes. Glenmore had the capacity to produce over one thousand different bourbons. It turned out that whiskey combined with laughter was good medicine, and the business stayed afloat during Prohibition years. The Tramp also stayed afloat, the party boat belonging to the company vice-president. The boat's swastika flag was a common sight on the Ohio River. Prior to the Nazis, the swastika was an ancient symbol meaning 'Good Luck.'

Many Owensboro businesses revolved around the 'medicinal' liquor industry, from whiskey barrel factories and saloons, to the red-light district on Mulberry Street. The Mulberry Street brothel offered Sunday beer along with prostitution. The business took a hit from Prohibition, but withstood the tough times. Sex on Mulberry Street survived the era and even peaked during World War II. During forty years of business, over one thousand women had 'worked' in the six brothels on the one street. Mulberry Street was later renamed Cedar Street perhaps when Dr. Seuss' first book, And to Think That I Saw it on Mulberry Street was released.

Chicago gangs had their own ways of adapting to Prohibition. The Bookie gang was a modern Robin

Hood operation stealing money from another gang's gambling ventures. It took a thief to know one. The money trail was easy for a crook to follow and funnel elsewhere. The Irish leader of the Bookie gang was the sharp dressed "Bugs" Moran. "Bugs" was short for 'buggy,' which meant crazy. Judges knew him not only for the crimes he committed, but for his sense of humor. He was once seen roller skating with one hand on his wife and a pistol on the other.

Matters took a serious turn when Chicago's North side clashed with the South side over crime turf. No one laughed when the term, 'drive-by shooting' was coined. Al "Scarface" Capone's rival gang allegedly ambushed Bugs Moran's Bookie gang during what would later be called the Valentine's Day Massacre on February 14, 1929. Capone's men dressed like cops and gunned down seven members of Moran's gang at a Lincoln Park garage in Chicago.

Thirty-nine bullets were fired to kill seven men, including the garage mechanic. His dog was left unharmed, chained to the bumper. Moran was also unharmed, arriving to the shootout five minutes late. He survived, but his stranglehold on Chicago's North side did not. After losing the power struggle to Capone, Moran moved to a safe house in none other than Owensboro, Kentucky. Formerly called Millionaire Row, Moran's new residence on Littlewood Drive would later become a part of Owensboro's Dogwood Azalea Trail. Bugs chose this trail in the Big O to live incognito.

He rented the house on Littlewood from a vacationing couple. Owensboro was less imposing than Chicago, but a place where everybody wanted to know your name. Neighbors kept tabs on the newcomer Moran who posed as an oil dealer. Some neighbors kept count of how many milk bottles were delivered to the rental home in one day. Neither the Mob, nor the Feds, had anything over nosy Owensboro neighbors who thought it quirky when Moran pulled into vacant parking slots to let cars pass before entering his own driveway.

One neighbor was especially in the know when it came to Moran. His home on the Dogwood Trail was used as an FBI headquarters to trail the gangster. For four months, agents took twelve hour shifts tracking Moran's comings and goings through the dining room window of this neighbor's home. The family continued to occupy their home along with the FBI agents. When the children asked about the live-in strangers, their dad answered, "They're Bugs exterminators." (Keefe, p.328)

Eventually the Feds caught up with Moran after more petty robberies, and brought him to the Daviess County Jail in Owensboro. Moran was sentenced to serve his jail term at Kansas' Leavenworth prison. Within two weeks there, Moran died of lung cancer. It was not alcohol or gunfire which did the beer baron in; cigarettes were his bullets.

Unbelievably, Owensboro had another tie to Chicago's 1920's crime scene. The twisted tale began on the back roads in Owensboro, in Utica. The true story was literally made for the movies but best described through the song, Hula Lou-a song chosen by the murderess herself:

*I've got the cutest eyes never mind what shade they are." The accused murderess' eyes were cute enough to fool a jury of twelve men to be acquitted for a murder she admitted.

*"I'm the gal he'd never forget." The victim's four torturous hours dying in the gal's bed made a lasting impression.

*"I got more sweeties than a dog has fleas." The four men in her life stuck with her until either she died or they did.

*"I'm the gal who can't be true." This much was true and the reason she got into the murder business in the first place.

*"And I don't care how nasty I may be," which explained why she presumably copped a buzz sipping gin while Hula Lou played repeatedly as her lover died a slow death.

This Hollywood version of murder was made into the Broadway musical, Chicago. The saga was inspired by a true homicide with the character of Roxie Hart based on the real person of Beulah Sheriff, born in a country village of the Big O. Chicago could easily have been called 'Utica' after Beulah's birthplace, but it wasn't as catchy.

Beulah's real epic began when she married an Owensboro newspaper boy. Just fifteen years old, she blamed her parents for pushing her into the marriage.

Beulah could not help her situation, or the origin of her name. In Hebrew, Beulah's name meant 'married,' but did not refer to a wife. When used for a woman, Beulah meant lady-boss. Beulah lived up to her namesake when she disposed of her first young husband through divorce and remarried a mechanic who moved her to Chicago in 1920.

Beulah did not kill husband number one, two, three, or almost four. She was accused of killing a lover while still married to husband number two, the mechanic. She supposedly shot her lover in her marital bedroom while her mechanic husband toiled away at the garage. Afterwards, Beulah had a stout drink and watched her lover die for the next four hours before calling her husband.

While waiting for trial, Beulah met another accused murderess while playing beauty shop in jail. They discussed makeup, the latest hairstyles, gave each other manicures and pedicures, thus raising the bar for inmate fashion behind bars. Beulah received much fan mail while in Chicago's Cook County Jail, probably some from her Owensboro hometown.

She was accused of shooting her lover in the back while under the influence of drink and jazz. She used tipsiness, combined with the swoon of jazz, as a flimsy defense to portray herself as a fragile female. Her beauty defense worked as she batted her eyes at the all-male jury and powdered her nose between pouty sighs. It was too bad that murder wasn't skin deep.

Beulah created a fashionable murder movement. It could have been called "What would Beulah do?" The rate of women murdering men shot up four hundred percent during this time. Most were abusive husbands, but not in Beulah's case. Her victim was not even her husband, although the femme fatale was known as 'the husband killer.' The husband she cheated on stood by her side and provided her with the best lawyer a mechanic could buy. The jury only deliberated two hours and came back with a "not guilty" verdict.

On one day, Beulah was acquitted, and on the next, she divorced loyal husband number two who was "too slow." She chose a boxer as her next husband because she liked 'em quick on their toes, maybe fast enough to dodge bullets. But the boxer was not her speed either so she divorced him too and headed into the arms of another. It looked as if nothing could keep up with this Owensboro gal, but then tuberculosis took its toll on Beulah almost four years to the day of the murder she was accused of committing. Beulah wasted away the rest of her days in a sanatorium. Her beauty could defend her no more.

Four men mourned as her coffin was laid to rest at a Presbyterian church in Owensboro's Daviess County, where her life started. These men were either had-been husbands or gonna-be husbands. Curiously, Beulah's tombstone records her death a year earlier than when she actually died.

The two Big O cities seemed to move in concentric circles. I once thought of Chicago as the big league and little ol' Owensboro as glacially slow. Oh Puh-leeze! Mobsters, Mulberry Street, husband killer-our dogwoods and backwoods presented more drama than Hollywood.

3
LIVING ON THE EDGE

"Growin' up in the heartland." I chanted along with John Cougar's little ditty bout Jack and Diane. The old tune was playing somewhere, maybe just in my head. I immediately thought of my old Kentucky home. "'Growing up in the Heartland' would make a good book title," I said aloud.

"Are you talking to me?" my husband, Randy, asked from the next room.

"It might even make a good movie."

"What would it be about?" he asked.

I repeated, "Growing up in the Heartland." Where was my phone? I lifted up the Mount Olympus stack of papers on the desk but it was not underneath. I wanted to text my husband in the next room in order not to yell over the squealing dishwasher, although the annoying sound was not unbearable enough to wash dishes by hand. I physically walked to my husband to ask if he had seen my phone, and did not consider continuing the rest of our conversation face-to-face.

There it was behind the keyboard. The phone slurped with an incoming text from my husband. It read: Btw the Big O is not in the heartland, followed by a sad face Emoji. Sure it was. I grew up there and should know. "The heartland is like North and South Dakota," he shouted from the other room. I pretended not to hear over the dishwasher.

I could not picture the Dakotas as the heartland, for heartland sounded like a warm place. On the other hand, my hometown of Owensboro was smack dab in the middle of mainstream America and recently voted the All-American City. That would definitely make us the heartland, except instead of hot dogs and apple pie we preferred mutton and banana pudding.

Jack and Diane's little ditty was about Indiana. If Indiana was in the heartland, I knew we were. With land at stake, Kentucky would go neck and neck with the Hoosier State over heartland bragging rights with the same tenacity as we did in basketball. We were serious about basketball and hesitated to even call it a game. Owensboro contributed great basketball athletes like Cliff Hagan, Rex Chapman, and Rebecca Greenwell, thus living up to its name as Kentucky's number one sportstown. Every Kentucky child could spell 'horse' correctly, not from the Derby races, but from basketball games. All toddlers dribble, but Kentucky toddlers dribble basketballs.

Even when Indiana's former coach, Bobby Knight's face was ablaze with the same red color as the Hoosier uniform, the University of Kentucky's Big Blue never backed down from a good fight. I mean game. At the time, I was obsessed with UK's Kyle Macy. Following his every move on TV, I even rubbed my socks the way he did for good luck before shooting a free throw. When the Wildcats played Indiana, the basketball arena featured both free throws and chair throws. I was on pins and needles, waiting for Coach Knight to throw a chair at the referees. Wait for it, wait. Here it comes... I was never disappointed when he earned a big T from the referee. To witness his technical foul was almost as exciting as James Lee's slam dunk.

KYLE
KYLE MACY SENIOR GUARD
UNIVERSITY OF KENTUCKY BASKETBALL WILDCATS

Randy would not let the heartland topic go though. "I'd check a map before I wrote a whole book about living in the Heartland."

I checked online for his peace of mind. The first search for America's heartland brought up a bunch of shoes for sale. I refined the search and finally a United States map appeared with the heartland states covered in red. There sat a cardinal colored Indiana on the computer screen glaring back at me with puffed up heartland status. Indiana was in the heartland, according to this map. North and South Dakota were not. And neither was Kentucky.

"Hey look. My home state of Illinois is in the heartland," my husband said as he walked past the screen. All this time, almost fifty years, I believed I had grown up in the heartland of America while living in Owensboro, Kentucky. I couldn't write a book called Growing up Beneath Indiana. I was crushed. I wanted to throw my chair.

4

CHILDREN OF THE CORN

I told myself I would remember this day for the rest of my life. It was a Wednesday. Never mind the date. Four-year-olds had no business with dates. I was tired of not remembering things that had happened to me, interesting things like the seahorse ride and bumper boats at Santa Claus Land, and an earthquake which toppled the ninety-nine bottles of wine on the wall at Grandmother and Papa's liquor store. There would be more Santa Claus Lands in my future, but one could never tell with earthquakes.

Vietnam protests rang in the year I was born. Simon and Garfunkel may have recorded Sounds of Silence for that reason. I was too young to recall the rioters in fashionable mini-skirts, but I vaguely remembered Walter Cronkite droning, "And that's the way it is."

Born in the late sixties, my birth was timed with Pampers' new disposable diapers. Mom never got the memo because she still used bunny-shaped diaper pins when my baby brother was born. I loved to wind my brother's baby swing with the loud crank which startled him and made us both scream. I never dreamed he would stay with our family in our two bedroom trailer as our home was already bursting at the seams. We at least had our own rooms while Mom and Dad slept on the pullout couch in the living room.

Like any other day, I threw open the trailer's spring door and hopped off the front stoop of lot #6. I played in the front yard since the back of our trailer was practically on the railroad tracks. The rails were a much used highway for trains headed to the steel mill just past the overpass.

Trains were a much-hailed event as I watched from the marigold flowerbed I wasn't allowed to go past. I anticipated the conductor's wave first and waited for the coal cars to pass before spying the guy on the caboose. He waved with one hand and exaggerated falling off the train for my entertainment. For all I knew, he could have been a hobo who hopped the train. If he fell for real, I would have laughed like I was supposed to do.

Night trains were my nightlights. Their search lights lit up the contents of my bedroom so I was not afraid of the dark. When the glare shone on the bedroom dresser, my lone goldfish sloshed in his round bowl. Between the trains' spotlights and Owensboro's only city lights from the steel mill, my nights were just like day.

The mill's smokestacks rose up behind the trailer, continuously puffing smoke billows. In a Biblical sense, the steel mill provided a pillar of light by night and pillar of cloud by day. I loved playing outside, under the steam-filled sky. Because there was always something new to explore on our trailer lot, I first checked under the trailer, just in case the turtle had come back. I had nurtured and adored him for one day until he mysteriously disappeared.

I was humming "Jeremiah was a bullfrog" and decided to name my next frog, Jeremiah for the upcoming frog race my cousins held at Memaw's house. I never had good luck with frogs. Mine either played dead or wished they were. Besides, I believed the frogs were responsible for my warts. I had nine lumps on my right knee as proof.

I kicked my tricycle aside and was ready for a big girl bike with a banana seat. Nita and Norma, in the next trailer, had practiced teaching me to ride a bicycle. The two ladies doted on my brother and me. Nita told my mother, "Michelle doesn't run; she floats." The thought lasted until she saw me ride a bike. As soon as Dad came home from work, we would try again. The training wheels were not going back on, even if it meant skinning my other knee with the warts on them. I stared down at one red-streaked knee and blew on the Merthiolate medicine stain out of pure habit. It still stung, probably a symptom of acute mercury poisoning before the medicine with the skull and crossbones label was banned. We didn't have Dora the Explorer Band-Aids to hide the fact we fell off a bike.

The other trailer park kids already rode solo without a parent chasing behind their bikes. The secret was to keep pedaling so you didn't tip over. Tire marks lined the curb and marked accident scenes where plenty of out-of-control bicycles skidded to a halt. I had no choice but to join the other victims and learn to ride unless I wanted to hear, "Baby, Baby, suck your thumb, wash it out with bubblegum."

When the others teased, I boasted that I could drive. It was true; I could drive before I was five. It was easier to steer our baby blue Volkswagen through the trailer park than it was to steer my bike. Dad often let me sit on his lap to drive. He worked the pedals while I did most of the driving work. The only bad thing about the Volkswagen was that it had no air-conditioning. Otherwise, it was a child's playground. You could sit on the floorboard and pretend that the backseat was a track for Matchbox cars. Or, you could stand in the middle of the car in the space between the front bucket seats and plead in Mom's ear, "I have to go to the bathroom." The pull-down seat cushion in the middle allowed you to see out the triangle windows which rolled out. And the little cubby hole under the rear windshield was perfect for taking naps. A Volkswagen was like a children's play fort, except it was moving. The only difference between it and the playground was that once you stopped playing, you were in a brand new place.

While sitting cross-legged in the grass, I picked at my knee scab until it bled again. Restless, I plucked a sprig of grass and wondered who named it bluegrass. It didn't look blue to me. But I loved the way the tiny shoot felt when I pulled the root without breaking the blade. The grass went directly into my mouth to chew, but didn't taste as good as the sour grass at Grandmother's house. Bored, I searched for dandelions to blow and spent hours making wishes in the wind with all the weeds in the yard. I left the white clover weed alone because it was a bee magnet, just as I was. The abandoned Dixie cup was lying in the weeds, but I figured I had gotten as much mileage out of my plastered arm as I could.

I had earned two bee stings in my elbow crease, which only hurt if I bent my arm. Trapping bees under a Dixie cup was pure fun, especially when the bees got good and mad enough to sting you when you released them. Mom would make a baking soda paste and force me to drink grape Kool-Aid. The war wounds were a great attention grabber and a joy to show off to friends. Before long, they too, were stung by bees. And scientists wondered where all the bees went.

I was pleased with how I looked then. With a Merthiolate stained knee, bruised shin, and two bee stings, I was tattooed red, white, and blue. I declared this day to be the day I would start remembering everything that happened to me for the rest of my life. Other than my patriotic coverings, the only other thing that caught my eye was a piece of farm equipment, a combine in the corn fields across the highway. Reid's Apple Orchard was just past the field, but I wasn't able to see the trees for the corn. How do you like them apples? I liked mine just like Grandmother did, with salt on them.

Grandmother and Papa visited our trailer once a week. When their car pulled into the narrow drive, I ran to the bathroom and strained. Papa had an idea to curtail my many trips to the doctor for constipation. He paid me a dollar every time I went to the bathroom. It was my 'duty' to perform once a week for a George Washington.

Our trailer park was surrounded by corn. If it weren't for the train tracks, the corn would stalk our back door. The corn only stopped at the Ohio River. It had always been like that even from the time that Owensboro's first settler, William Smothers, was in the '1803 Corn Stalk Militia' according to the historical marker. Owensboro's Daviess County ranked third in the state for corn production. It was hard to imagine anywhere else in the tri-state having more corn than we did. Ironically, Barren County had the most fertile land in the state, despite its name.

That afternoon I sat alone in the bluegrass while staring at the golden corn. A small stretch of sky rose above the field, and as I looked into the cauliflower clouds, I pledged aloud: "I am Michelle (just in case I changed names in the future) and I am four years old. I will always remember the combine in this corn field."

I ran inside to ask Mom what year it was so I could document it. I wished I hadn't. I got the answer I needed, 1970, but Mom was reminded I needed a nap, although I thought I was too old for daily naps. No one would tell me I was too young to remember when I was four years old though. I felt smug with myself and proud that most four year olds didn't even know what a combine was.

5

FLOWER CHILD

Recently a Facebook friend posted a picture of our kindergarten class. How was it that I remembered all thirty students from over forty years ago, but could only remember three of my current neighbors' names? I was a member of the afternoon kindergarten class, so I did not spend a great portion of my life there, yet I remember it as if it were yesterday.

Joey was next to me in the class picture because he was my shadow. If I was at the sand box, he was there. When we circled around the French speaking nun, Joey was the first to say, "Bonjour" to me. When we sat in our little wooden chairs after recess, he was there...except for the time when Joey went berserk.

It was the time he overthrew the class by overturning the other children's chairs, with them in it. Classmates were splayed on the floor and cried out of shock more so than pain. The wooden child-sized chairs were close to the ground already, so no child had a terribly long fall. But one moan led to a dull roar until the entire classroom droned like a swarm of angry bees.

I sat sheepishly in my stable chair while my kindergarten class was downsized, reduced to the floor. Joey left my chair untouched until I was the lone sitter. His dark brown eyes searched for approval in my blue ones. There appeared to be a motive for his random rampage; Joey liked me. Joey's escapade topped any future attempts of boys to win my heart. No boy ever went to such lengths to get my attention, putting me above all else…literally.

Joey and I in Kindergarten class picture

As Joey ran from the teachers, words from a popular song popped into my head: "Run Joey, Joey run-run the hounds are on your trail." Hounds could be substituted with nuns. Even Sister Judy was uprooted from her chair. Boy is he going to get it now. But instead of Sister Judy joining Joey on the run, she waited until his energy waned and calmly escorted him from the room.

The whining died instantly as all ears were pricked to listen for any signs of a struggle or Joey pleading for mercy. But when Sister and Joey returned, there were no signs of remorse. Instead, Joey's eyes twinkled as they caught mine and he grinned from ear to ear. If I were among the fallen students, I would not have been satisfied with the kindergarten justice system.

Years later I learned that Joey had a growth disorder and teachers knew he was a sick little boy. I prayed for Joey even after he died. I could still picture Joey's maniacal smile and his chest heaving up and down while he staged the mutiny for my benefit. He had nothing to lose after his tirade. His grin revealed it was worth it.

After the school day, Mom drove the old Volkswagen to Memaw's house. Papaw lived there too and even built the clapboard frame home, but we still called it Memaw's house. The fragrance of brewed coffee met us at the door. Sometimes the home smelled of Vick's Vapor Rub, the musky salve used to coat our congested chests when we coughed. Memaw believed a warm pair of socks kept a cough away in the first place, but socks were hard to come by since most were made into cute sock monkeys with long tails. If Vick's didn't cure a cough, it was time to bring in the big guns. Whiskey or bourbon silenced the uncooperative cough after the victim passed out.

A cuckoo clock hung above the television set, which was as big as the kitchen stove. In Memaw's kitchen, a lacquered table awaited us with tall Tupperware salt and pepper shakers as centerpieces. A deep sink filled with soapy McCoy dishes awaited whoever cared to notice. The piano and grandfather clock were the only pieces I remembered in the dark living room since the blinds were pulled to keep rowdy children out. In contrast, a doorway from the living room led to Memaw's bright bedroom with its white chenille bedspread, the kind that left marks on your face when you fell asleep. The rotary telephone was just outside the bedroom door. We couldn't answer the ring unless it was "ours." The party line had certain rings for certain neighbors. Grandkids laughed when Papaw answered "ours" with, "Yell-o."

Memaw was usually in her flower garden or canning butter pickles. From her, I learned the names of plants like the iris, daffodils, Johnny jump-ups, and the mimosa tree whose pink flowers floated across the highway. Memaw rarely picked her flowers unless they were for the May Procession. Each May, young girls decorated a Maypole with flowers for the special church service. The poles were refurbished canes from ring-toss wins at the annual picnic, covered in tin foil, with flowers attached. May Processions were still a passed down tradition. Back in Memaw's day, May queens wore dresses made of paper, like paper dolls. I picked flowers anytime I could to make daisy chains, which were actually made from weeds, not daisies. The hobby transformed into gum wrapper chains, macramé necklaces with fancy beads from Maglinger's, and hanging pots of jute-all of which represented the hippy times in the seventies.

Papaw once owned a tenor guitar. Fellow band members would pick him up with a horse and buckboard every weekend for picnic gigs in Indiana. Papaw's guitar made him a lot of money back then, $2 a gig. When his band played, folks joined in the fun with barn dancing. The time that Memaw joined the fun and danced with someone else was the last time Papaw played with the band. The tenor guitar disappeared, and no one mentioned it again.

So now, everything belonged to Memaw except for Papaw's grape arbor, which wrapped around the porch. Vines separated the concrete patio from the graveled drive and shaded the porch glider where I scratched Papaw's back and petted Frisky the dog. Sometimes Papaw took us for a ride up the lane in the back of his pick-up truck. Afterwards, I picked green grapes before they ripened and was sorry I did. The back of my throat puckers when I think of those sour grapes. I told Papaw then, "Did you know they have grapes at the store with no seeds in them?" It was a revelation to me and I thought he ought to know.

The early seventies was a time when the flower children were having children of their own. Lady Bird Johnson inspired America's beautification with wildflowers by the roadside. Signs along the highway did not specify speeding fines, but emphasized the fines for littering. To be called a litterbug was the worst insult. "Give a hoot, don't pollute, never be a dirty bird" was advertised daily on WVJS and WOMI radios.

On the drive back to the trailer park, we passed more gardens belonging to little old ladies. Their gardens showcased real flowers mixed with plastic ones and reflective pinwheels. I loved flowers of all kinds, even fake ones that spun in the breeze. Once, I stole some plastic florets and 'planted' them next to the railroad tracks. My green thumb was caught red-handed stealing flowers. I was forced to uproot them and return the stems to the little old lady.

Shoplifting plants has always been a touchy subject for me. Even as an adult, when filling out six pages of personal information for a Master Gardener background check, I sweated the results. My neighbor received her confirmation before mine, and I worried it was because I deadheaded plants at Home Depot while confiscating the extra seeds or 'helping the flowers' at the Botanical Garden by pinching them back. I could not help it if the seeds fell into my hands, but I kept handy envelopes in my purse just in case. My personal flower garden is a horticultural zoo with two of every kind of plant, just in case I see an ark being built.

Unlike Kindergarten, first grade was a blur with only two instances I recalled. One was of our class singing "Go tell Aunt Rhody the old gray goose is dead." The song still makes me yawn. Perhaps the lyrics were used to inspire the school board to invest in a real music program. By the time I reached eighth grade, we were singing Rockin' Robin.

There was also the time I almost lost my right hand. In the cafeteria, I sat next to my best friend, Kimberly. When she turned her back, I swiped her dill pickle. Flowers were not the only things I lifted. She tried to pry the pickle from my curled fingers and fit my fist into her mouth. As she gnawed on my hand, the pickle fell to the floor. I carried my maimed hand with my other hand to show the bite marks to my teacher. To my dismay, my former friend went scot-free and I was made to stand in the corner for stealing food. I lost that food fight.

I thought I was in America and not some place where they cut off your hand for stealing. I did not see my friend for years after transferring to a new school. We eventually came back together in high school. She went by the name of Kim, but I knew who she was. She instinctively shielded her food from me and I shielded my appendages. Thankfully I still have use of my right hand.

Peace signs were a sign of the times then, from iron-on blue jean patches to bumper stickers. We were expected to live in peace at home while praying for peace in Russia too. To me, keeping the peace meant keeping my hands to myself.

6

THE BRIDGES OF DAVIESS COUNTY

When I thought of bridges, three words came to mind: I hated them. Not every bridge, just the ones over water. I grew up with the superstitious notion of holding my breath over bridges until I realized I would need every ounce breath if I accidentally went off the bridge.

On some bridges, I not only held my breath, but closed my eyes until the bridge ordeal was over. It was not about getting over the bridge; it was more about the bridge getting over with. Fortunately I was not the driver when I had to squeeze my eyes shut.

If it weren't for Miller's Lake with its slides and swinging trapezes as the end destination, I would never have crossed the wooden bridge to get to it. During the Great Depression era, the construction of the recreational lakes was the best thing to happen to the economy when a farmer employed locals to dig the fishing lakes and build cabins from the surrounding poplar trees.

Miller's Lake was the best thing to happen to me, since I finally passed beginner swim lessons at the Sportscenter pool. The sixth time was the charm because of the darned rhythmic breathing. Mom worried that the guards finally promoted me because I towered over the little kids in my beginner class. It only appeared that way because I was so skinny. I also failed to float on my back, but over the years, the back float became my best stroke. Fat floated. It was Mom who insisted I learned to swim because she never learned herself. Plus, Owensboro was a river town, surrounded by water.

Miller's Lake was my favorite place with paddle boats and miniature golf. I was only disappointed once, when we drove all the way there just to find it was closed for the season due to head lice. Lice was not enough to stop me from burying my brother in the sand, but the old wooden bridge to Miller's Lake made me think twice. It must have been built in the Depression era too. Yet, there I was as a passenger in my Aunt Charlotte's car every summer. A stop sign before the bridge prepared me for the giant breath I would have to take in order to cross it.

Cars crept slowly over the old bridge to hear every splinter crack and feel every board wobble. One time, Aunt Charlotte's car stopped so I thought that bridge was over and opened my eyes. To my horror, we were stalled in the middle of the bridge with muddy water swishing below. I screamed until we reached dry land and then kissed the gritty sand at Miller's Lake.

Another bridge over the same creek gave me similar conniption fits. Luckily, this bridge was past St. Martin's Church, so I didn't whine about it when it came time for the annual church picnic. Oh how I loved the picnic which included a cake walk, ring-toss over Coke bottles and canes, and the homemade burgoo with standing room only. Burgoo was a special Kentucky stew which rhymed with 'thank you,' not bird doo. Makeshift bars without stools were built for fast food consumption. After you stood in line, you stood to eat too. I would have braved that bridge rather than skipping the picnic's burgoo bar or missing midnight Mass at the church there.

Every Christmas Eve, Mom played the church organ from St. Martin's choir loft. I joined in the chorus for O Holy Night and Let There Be Peace on Earth. The two hymns ushered in good will toward men and brought forth a dusting of snow at the same time. Snowflakes sprinkled the faithful just as Mass ended. 'Twas the season to be grateful for magical moments as this and for the fact the Panther Creek Bridge was on the south side while we were on the north. While this bridge was not wooden, the creek frequently flooded with rotten wood passing closely below. The bridge was often washed out with water clear up to the railing.

Growing up on the banks of the Ohio, bridges were everywhere, all with water underneath. Daily I passed over the one lane bridge on Carter Road since my Memaw and Papaw lived in Rome, outside of Owensboro. The bridge was set at an angle, so a one lane diagonal bridge made my phobia worse. Cars made a mad dash to see which could get to the bridge first. Because we went eighty miles per hour over it, I did not have to hold my breath for long. If Dad drove, my stomach dropped as it did when the car flew over hilltops. My brother and I laughed afterwards. He did so because of the anti-gravity feeling and I laughed because

I was alive.

For years, a white wooden cross was raised next to a pole after the bridge. Memaw took care of that cross when mowers moved it or it blew down. It was in memory of her son who died in a car wreck when I was four years old. Only the cross was left for Memaw to care for. The ditches on either side of that bridge claimed two more relatives' lives. One of those was my cousin, Tommy, taken right before Christmas. Outside of losing those dear to me, there was no love lost between me and Carter Road's big ditches.

There were still more bridges to cross. From the curved riverbank, Owensboro stared at the main bridge that spanned the Aquarius between Kentucky and Indiana. Technically called the Glover Cary Bridge, locals took control of the name game and christened that bridge based on its color. We aptly called it the blue bridge. The big blue bridge was supposed to blend in with the blue sky above, blue grass across, and the blue water below.

Our skies were frequently blue, but not canary blue like our bridge. Nothing in nature was that blue. It looked like a toy Lego bridge before it received a toned-down paint job. Some voted for an even bluer bridge of turquoise, as if it could get any bluer. Owensboro made a good color choice and stuck with basic blue.

The city rested at the river's bend. Shaped like a crescent roll, it was a well-rounded town. New Orleans claimed the Crescent City name already, so Owensboro chose to be the Festival City instead. Arguably, we could have conjured up a Bourbon Street and re-enlisted Owensboro's old street cars if we wanted to steal the Crescent City's thunder. Thunder on the Ohio was already in our roots.

Owensboro used to be called Owensburough, named after Col. Abraham Owen who was killed in the Battle of Tippecanoe. Owen was a worthy military officer and Kentucky statesman, yet never lived in Owensboro. Our town chose names based on merit and residency was not a requirement.

Names were mostly chosen by color scheme. The riverbank was so yellow that Owensboro was originally named Yellow Banks. The Ohio River looked green to me, but a Green River already flowed nearby and one should not confuse the two. In my mind, I had burned Calhoun's Bridge over the Green River already because of the time when one lane was closed with mere traffic cones separating cars from the gaping hole to the river below. I became acutely aware of just how much my tires were out of alignment. The Green River Bridge was not for me. Nevertheless, a river between Kentucky and Indiana should not be called the Ohio. It was no wonder we resorted to naming city parts, like our bridge, from a paint-by-number chart.

Perhaps the worst bridge was in Friendly Village. Don't let the name fool you. A swinging bridge swung over the same ol' Panther Creek. I dared to walk across the rickety crossing once. When I was over the middle of the creek, my friend's brother gave the roped bridge a few extra swings by jumping on it. I held on for my life and didn't notice the rope burns on my palms until I was on dry land. After the swinging episode, I was not friendly and didn't care which village I was in.

Dad often preached parables dealing with peer pressure and the penalties of following the crowd. He used bridges in his homily for effect. "If everyone else jumped off a bridge, would you?" That's when the comparison backfired. A team of racehorses couldn't make me jump off a bridge.

I wondered if one really ever got over Gephyrophobia, the real fear of bridges. I made progress this past summer when I walked across the great blue bridge on Bridge Day. I crossed to Indiana and back, without making a splash. Facing my fear, I stopped in the middle of the bridge to gape over the edge. That didn't bother me as much as the little drainage holes on the pavement did. I could see the river rippling below through those circular peepholes. My shoe fit through one of them, and I had to tell myself that the rest of my body would not realistically fit. Tell that to my beating heart.

Still, it was a big step for my little shoe. Maybe if I could pinpoint where my fear first began, it would help. Mom worried that she passed her bridge phobia onto me. When she was young, she and her brothers rode bikes down Hayden Bridge Road (already sounded scary), and crawled down into a culvert, under an old wooden bridge. She and her siblings would lie in wait until a car passed over. They remained under the bridge even as the rupturing sounds of the see-saw planks warped under the weight of a car while the entire bridge sagged. This could have been when Mom's fear of bridges began. I would say she was right.

Life with bridges was interesting. Although Owensboro's main bridge was funded under FDR's New Deal, some remember that it was a toll bridge until 1954. That was before it was blue; it used to be silver. Back then, anything could come across if it had correct change. Instead of banning pedestrians, the sign read: Pedestrians and bicycles not allowed on bridge unless going entirely across. MUST PAY TOLL. Pedestrians 10 cents, Bicycles 25 cents. Wheels or feet didn't matter. If it moved, it paid. Bicycles rode along with vehicles, tractors, or whatever. Safety wasn't included in the price and you crossed at your own risk. No lifeguard on duty either.

7

ANOTHER FACE IN THE CROWD

In the 1970s, townspeople flocked to a liquid race track on the river during the yearly Regatta. I cheered for either the Atlas Van Lines or Miss Budweiser sponsored hydroplanes for the sole reason that they usually won.

It was just the two of us, Dad and I, who enjoyed the hydroplanes. We liked races of all sorts, especially stock car races at the Kentucky Motor Speedway in Whitesville. As a proud member of the Darrell Waltrip Fan Club, I watched Darrell beat everyone, every time, every weekend. "Boogity, Boogity, let's go racing boys and girls!" I never turned down a chance to go to the track for a demolition derby. And I never dreamed I would double-date with his younger brother, also a racecar driver.

Racing hydroplanes fell into the same sports category of fast and loud. The blaring of the engines travelled as high up as the Western Kentucky Gas platform on the riverbank from where we watched. My dad's company had a knack for staking out the best vantage points for city-wide events like Regattas and parades. For the Christmas parade, we were in a good position, but I still wanted Dad to hold me on his shoulders so Santa would notice I was there. It made it easier for Santa's elves to hand me a candy cane without stooping. I was only endangered by motorcycle figure eights when the Shriners zoomed so close that I felt the swooshing of their Fez tassels.

The Regatta was a similar experience, with masses of people weaving in and out. Those on the gas company's three-story platform stood out from the multitude with their binoculars. The scaffolding was like what a painter would use. We shimmied up the outside of the framework for a Kentucky Cardinal's view of the race. I could see Indiana from the stand just as well as Sarah Palin could see Russia from her house. From on high, the hydroplanes looked like water bugs zipping on top of a murky swimming pool.

After the hydroplanes whirred in circles for several intervals much like the Shriners, the droning ceased. The air continued to ring even after the engines rested. My eardrums still hissed like the waves. The half-time show was not on a field, but on the river itself. Everyone pointed to the bridge. Patrol boats darted from the towers underneath the bridge while divers in frog gear scanned the water.

At the same time, a lone figure walked to the middle of the bridge. The crowd chanted, "Jump. Jump. Jump!" This wasn't a ruthless crowd, but they were expecting a show. The man was a stunt jumper and the jump was planned. The audience cheered as if they were at Sea

World and the jumper was Shamu.

My dad was quickly by my side to shield my eyes. Not only could I not hear, but then I couldn't see. Dad must have thought I would try it at home. I peeked through his fingers and spied the jumper climbing over the bridge railing. A hush fell over the crowd as it waited and waited and waited.

Alas, the water was too choppy. No jump. The adventure-rushed crowd was audibly disappointed after holding their breaths for so long. They held their breaths for nothing like I did when it came to bridges.

Forty years later, I stroll along the same Smothers Park many now call the River Park, and climb a newly constructed lookout. It is one of the only concrete trees in Kentucky, maybe even in America. I side-step a concrete possum too, if ever there was a doubt I was in Kentucky. I love my old Kentucky home with its recent face-lift and yellow bank makeover, concrete and all.

The water spouts encircling me make me feel so alive, as if I am young again and back on the gas company's Regatta platform. From the current treetop loft, I have the same panoramic view of the river, like I did back then. The view is tangible proof of what $120 million can buy. I believe this spot to be the exact piece of ground from where I watched the Regatta stunt jumper who didn't jump. My surroundings are based on the position of the blue bridge, except it had been silver then. I hoped color was the only change and that the bridge had not moved since then.

I now watched the river's crest rise and fall like humpbacked whales, reminding me of Sea World. The thought triggered a memory from the seventies, back to the Regatta scaffolding with the same view. I imagined hearing the raucous crowd over the hydroplanes and pictured a person about to jump from the bridge. Suddenly, a buzzer sounds and a crash of water makes me reach for the playground rails. The rushing water of the scheduled waterfall sounds as if someone has plunged into the water for real, but today, it was a controlled avalanche and I was the only one who did not expect it.

When the new waterfall calmed and the mist from the dancing fountains sprayed, the choking heat of August was stifled somewhat. I scanned Smothers Park to where the Executive Inn or Big E once stood, with the remains of its Showroom Lounge balcony still claiming part of the river. I had watched many shows there starring Owensboro's own, Florence Henderson of the Brady Bunch, Engelbert Humperdink, and alas, the famous Van Dells. I was among the countless females who lined up to kiss Steve Ricks when he impersonated Elvis. The

King was not alive anymore, or maybe this really was him. Good golly, I didn't own an alligator purse, but I bought a blue dress for when the fake Elvis sang Devil with a Blue Dress on.

A new Hampton Inn replaced Owensboro's former glory hotel, the Executive Inn. It would be a tough act to top, based on my fond memories of the former Big E. I wondered if the new hotel offered a buffet every Saturday night with crab legs, frog legs, and baked Alaska. Would the waitress instinctively know to bring me a Shirley Temple and Hearts of Palm salad while I waited in the buffet line? After dinner, could I ride a see-through elevator to the seventh floor and drop things from the top floor into the roofless gift shop? Finally, would the indoor heated pool reek of chlorine and wilt my Farrah Fawcett bangs as I walked past? I had great expectations for a hotel on the same site.

The new inn looked promising with a promenade area connecting it to the main path weaving along the river. The hotel's parking lot was where I remembered the city jail to have been. It was a parking lot with a jail in the middle of it. The old jail had once been a roomy historical home until city officials got the idea to lock-up criminals in its plentiful rooms. The house-turned-jail served as a median in the middle of the asphalt. You could drive on either side of it, much like a drive-thru, although the inmates didn't think so.

I remembered a class trip down by the jail one time. I vividly recalled strolling past the inmates while drinking my canned Dr. Pepper and toting my brown bag bologna lunch. The best part of field trips was getting out of school. The second best thing was removing the tin foil from sodas, which was supposed to keep them cold, and then spraying them 'accidentally.' It made it worth the trip-worth more to me than the three-hour Gandhi movie our class had watched.

I would not want to miss seeing the prisoners through barred windows with their fingers wrapped around the grills either. Every child secretly wished to see bad behavior punished and justice served, as long as it was not imposed on him or her. We expected the justice system to work like it did in our school institution.

We were in luck. The prisoners hurled obscenities at both teachers and school children as we passed. We weren't allowed to say anything in return, but it was still exciting. I didn't mind the name calling. Keep it up and you'll stay in there longer. That's what my parents always said to me when I was punished to my room. I came out of my jailbird reverie when I heard Lynyrd Skynyrd's Freebird playing over the River Park's speakers.

The jail disappeared with the new construction. Like the old jail, the modern hotel's rooms were filled too. The river view had also changed. Owensboro designed its green spaces for practical use as well as aesthetic beauty. Knockout roses added color to the landscape while marsh grasses rustled in the breeze as if whispering secrets of the past. I took the time to listen.

My eyes focused on the common area in the middle of the grassy amphitheater, the new McConnell Plaza. This was the same ground where another platform was erected eighty Augusts ago. A different excited crowd anticipated a man to climb a platform and fall to his doom, although this event had nothing to do with a Regatta or the bridge. The mob gathering would not be disappointed in 1936, well before my time.

No Regatta buttons commemorated the 1936 occasion, but one-of-a-kind souvenirs were to be had, for sure. Folks clamored for the best view and came from all over to witness what was to be the last event of its kind in the country. The New York Times called the jamboree a Roman holiday. If my former neighbor, Winnie had been there in 1936, she could have said, "Hey, we have a festival for that!"

Food and ale were served in this festive atmosphere, but I doubted the offerings were as elaborate as fried chicken, pork chops, mashed potatoes, pickled cucumbers, cornbread, lemon pie and ice cream. For this was the last meal of the accused rapist, Rainey Bethea, on his last August morning.

The olden platform I had only seen in pictures was as rudimentary as the makeshift scaffolding I used to climb to watch the hydroplanes in my youth. But this particular decades-old structure was not meant to last over fifteen minutes. The public event drew a crowd even larger than later Regattas did. Some 20,000 people spent the night downtown in anticipation of the event at sunrise. Of those people, only seven of them were black. I wonder if that counted the eighteen-year old black man with a black hood over his head, hanging from the gallows while the dew was still wet.

Convicted criminal, Rainey Bethea, was hanged for raping a senior citizen. He had committed other heinous crimes, but it was the crime of rape which carried a gallows sentence in Kentucky at that time. Owensboro demanded the judgment with a female sheriff in charge. That was what all the hoopla was about.

Had I lived in Owensboro then, would I have seen the last public hanging in America? Chances are I might have attended. Many children were present with their parents in 1936. I might have had a good seat for the 'show' too. But I doubted my dad would have let me witness a noose knotted around a man's neck since I was not allowed to watch Charlie's Angels because Farrah was too pretty. Nor was I able to watch a stunt jumper who intended to jump.

The very pretty and the very ugly were not for my eyes. I could have spied the criminal taking off his shoes and putting on a new pair of socks. I could even have watched as Rainey Bethea stood on the trap door's X, which marked the spot where he would hang. But no, I definitely would not have seen the hanging corpse. It would be as if I had a hood over my face too.

8

WINNER TAKES ALL

"Ashes, ashes we all fall down!" One child failed to fall on cue and was yanked down by the group...hard. It was much easier to roll with it when playing Ring around the Rosies. Children had played this 'game' since the Great Plague in 1665, so one would think everyone would know the meaning of this rhyme by now.

However, I doubted my playgroup knew that rosies referred to rash and posies were bitter herbs to protect from the deadly rash. We certainly didn't know ashes were from the cremation process after contracting the Plague. "We all fall down" was what really happened when someone died.

Sometimes we played a courtship game, except we were six years old. At that age, we preferred to be the cheese that stood alone in the Farmer in the Dell. No one wanted to be the wife chosen by the blindfolded farmer. We did want to be the fair lady in London Bridge, not knowing she was a human sacrifice to hold up the bridge over the river Thames. We cheered and sang "Take a key and lock her up!"

We didn't know what we chanted. Most people probably don't. Skipping rope, where two people turned the rope while another jumped, had colorful words we sang in verse. Feet jumped and hearts pumped to "Cinderella dressed in yella." But sometimes we jumped to the rhythm of:

Lizzie Borden took an axe
And gave her mother forty whacks.
When she saw what she had done,
She gave her father forty-one.

Legend had it that Lizzie Borden axed her parents to death and she got away with murder. I was among the children around the world who sang about it.

Cowboys and Indians was our standby. One of us was a gunslinger with a plastic holster, and the other was a tomahawk thrower with a getaway horse tied up somewhere. We cried Indian war whoops when we found that Dad's hammer smashed the pink roll of caps on the sidewalk better than any gun did. Such was our 'big bang' theory.

For Owensboro forefathers, Cowboys and Indians was no game. To pioneers, 'game' meant something you shoot at in order to eat. Owensboro's first settler, William Smeathers, whose name was either butchered or made easier to spell when Owensboro wanted a Smothers Park named for a pioneer, found his father killed by Indians after a hunting expedition. Smothers' mother died of grief the same week. Legend had it that twelve-year old William devoted his life to hunting and killing Indians.

In his lifetime, William Smeathers (Smothers) fought several Indian campaigns along with Jim Bowie, the same Bowie of Alamo fame. When Smothers was found dead on a bearskin rug he had earned honestly, in his hand lay a tomahawk. Another contemporary of Smothers, Joe Daviess was shot by Indians-the Daviess for whom Owensboro's Daviess County was named. Over one hundred years later, we local children loved to smear war paint on cheeks and thought it was a great game. This was the game of life for generations before us.

Childhood games were rarely inclusive and progressed into survival of the fittest. Musical Chairs was especially competitive as players danced to music in a circle around chairs. With one less chair than there were players, the music stopped and players fought over limited chairs. This became a game for the biggest butts. Those who weren't well-endowed played with a handicap. Kids with bigger bottoms won the seats and made the skinny loser wish he had given up sooner.

Dodge ball was another game of skill. One player taunted with a ball while the rest of the group lined the wall like in a police lineup. The ball was aimed at the heads on the wall. If a person was hit and sunk to the ground, he received a ball as a consolation for his bloody nose, and became an additional thrower. When throwers outnumbered dodgers, it was akin to a stoning. It made more sense to be the first one thrown out instead of the last one standing.

Some games were mellow but involved mental bullying like Mother May I? If the player in charge didn't like another player, he meted out justice verbally. "You didn't say, 'Mother May I.'" This sent the least favorite person to the back of the pack until he quit. Tsk-tsk, winners never quit and quitters never win. Our games made sure of that.

Birthday parties had special games. Pin the Tail on the Donkey and the Egg in the Spoon Relay were two games I remember. Wheelbarrow races and balloon partner games were also birthday protocol. Games were designed to have winners and losers, with every winner receiving a prize. There was no point to winning if everyone received a prize. We did not sacrifice our awards to the birthday boy or girl, for we earned them fair and square. After winner took all, cake and ice cream were expected before gifts were opened. A cardboard container of vanilla ice cream with a wooden dipping stick was a perfect companion to chocolate cake.

Themed birthday parties became popular as the seventies progressed. Places like McDonalds and Dipper Dan's Ice Cream Parlor hosted our birthdays. We no longer played games, as long as we had the costumed Ronald McDonald and the Hamburglar to entertain us. Almost overnight, childhood games were no longer the main party events. Instead, we expected to be entertained while keeping our eyes on our fries.

9

1974

(Excerpts taken from *Tornado Valley: Huntsville's Havoc* by Shelly Van Meter Miller, Copyright 2012)

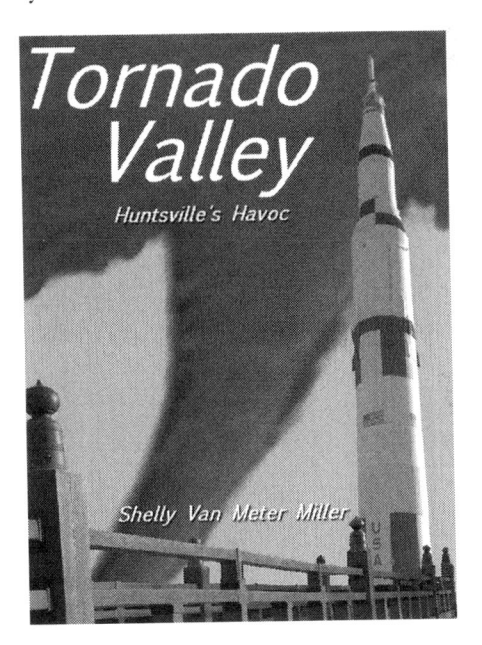

B irthdays were still a big deal, especially our country's 200th celebration. The United States prepared for its Bicentennial birthday years in advance. Red, white, and blue was the fashion, from bandanas to tube tops. When the two-dollar bill was introduced, Aunt Hazel practically bought out the Treasury. Until I was forty years old, I received the $2 gift from my aunt for every birthday. She did not believe in inflation. Leading up to the Bicentennial, teachers told us that we were lucky to participate in the 200th birthday of our country because we would not be alive for its next big birthday, the 300th year celebration.

Just like other little girls in the seventies, I assembled Barbie jets and swimming pools, and argued over who had to be Ken. I spent Saturday mornings watching cartoons, channeling through the only three stations on TV. I did this the old-fashioned way, by walking to the television and twisting a channel knob. For cartoons, the choices were Scooby-Doo, Shazam, or "Hey, Hey, Hey it's Fat Albert." Parents didn't worry about too much TV although they warned we would eventually go blind if we sat too close to the tube.

In 1974, a few things were scary like spiders, strangers, bridges, and tornadoes. I had encountered all except strangers and tornadoes. Therefore, I would remember the third day of April that year. It was the day the wind and whistles blew-an event that kids across thirteen states, and even Canada had in common.

The nightmare began while I was at school. The weather was unseasonably warm and we had spring fever. A common myth assured us that the Bon Harbor hills surrounding Owensboro protected us from twisters as long as we stayed away from the river. It was believed that tornadoes followed water. We'd heard of thunder on the Ohio.

We never cared about the weather unless it threatened daily recess. During dangerous weather, we stayed inside the classroom and played a quiet game of 7-up at our desks. Much like dodge ball, you ducked your head and a player tapped you, usually slugged you, on your head. Your job was to guess who had smacked you. That day, the storms were so menacing that we played 7-up all afternoon, foregoing our daily cleaning routine of banging chalk erasers together outside. With the lashing winds and the rain coming down in heavy sheets, the outdoors all but disappeared. All heads popped up when a crack of lightning caused the fluorescent lights to flicker, followed by a deafening boom of thunder. Game over.

The principal's voice trembled over the PA system as she commanded students to proceed single file into the interior hallway. We were escorted to the nuns' convent next door to the school, but not before each teacher blew a shrill whistle to herd us like cattle. We had practiced tornado drills before and were told to curl up into a ball with arms wrapped around our heads. Everyone was so rattled by the real deal that even the most conscientious tattle-tale hall monitor neglected his tornado duties during all the commotion.

He forgot to open the windows before assuming the tornado pose. It was believed that if the windows were cracked open, a tornado couldn't crack them. This was supposed to prevent our school from flying into another state, like Kansas, where Munchkins might say, "You're not in Kentucky anymore." We milked this window myth by rushing to lift the sashes during the height of extreme weather. The idea that vented windows released pressure was not true. We were virtually blown away by the truth later in life, much like when we learned that Pluto was not a planet.

Teachers continued to blow the whistles strapped around their necks. They blasted them intermittently into our eardrums as we passed. Kids held their ears in agony from the penetrating whistle sounds, coupled with wind gusts that thrashed against the school. We were rushed, but told not to hurry. The incongruent non-verbal signals created more panic. Anytime teachers displayed a false sense of calm, something bad was about to happen. The storms pounded our elementary school. I eyed the bathroom uneasily as I walked past, but I remained in the horde of students with bebop shoes clickety-clacking to the nuns' quarters. The nuns took quick baby steps in their long dresses. School nuns were always in full nun attire, like Sally Field in The Flying Nun. As much as I enjoyed the TV show, this was one day that I did not want to see a nun fly.

Our only source of communication with the outside world was a transistor radio, which announced when a tornado was on the ground. A tornado warning was only issued when someone actually witnessed it and alerted the radio station with, "Incoming!" Inevitably, the school lost power and kids shrieked in the dark. The nuns were prepared with candles and always seemed to know who was causing a commotion, as if they had eyes in the back of their habits. The convent wall was stone-cold concrete. I flinched away from it, not knowing if it was wet or just icy cold. The candlelight caused shadows to flicker across the walls so that the nuns' habits loomed larger than life and appeared to be floating around the convent. It would have been better to have kept my eyes closed.

Peculiar thoughts raced through my head. I wanted to see where the nuns slept because I often had wondered if nuns actually slept. I also worried because I had forgotten to wear shorts under my uniform dress. Just the week before, the nuns broke out the rulers to measure skirt lengths. Girls were sent home if the hem rose more than two inches above the knees. I made it through the previous week without growing, so I was probably okay on my knees for the potential tornado. My Army green knee socks were touching my face as I hugged them.

I did not want to be in a dark convent with wailing students and numerous nuns chanting the rosary at different intervals. As the nuns' invocations became more insistent, I realized that situations like these were probably where the statement, "You'd better say your Hail Marys" came from.

I encountered another problem while on my knees. When I murmured, "No, no, don't come," the other kids, who were hunched next to me, probably thought I was worried about the approaching tornado. I was, but I also worried about wetting my pants, like I did in first grade when making my first Confession. Instead of fight or flight, my body peed when under stress.

God may have forgotten my first grade sins, but I did not forget my first grade Confession. That day, I had wished school would dismiss before my turn. I prayed more about being saved by the bell than being saved from Hell. When I walked the line to the little closet where I would confess the sins of a six-year old, I entered the claustrophobic closet and left the door cracked. Immediately, a nun kicked it shut, squashing my only sliver of light. I groped around in the blackness on hands and knees while searching for the kneeler. I thought I heard soft murmurings coming from the closet next to mine, but my heart was pounding too loudly.

Snap! A sliding screen flew open between the booths. I saw the priest's moving lips, so I babbled on cue, "Bless me Father for I have…peed." The missing word was supposed to be "sinned" but I felt a warm gush spray down my legs and puddle around my kneeling knees. Not only had I sinned, I had peed in my pants.

I finally lived down the humiliation of first grade, but third grade was different. Children would not forget if I wet my pants again. So two years later, I huddled in a convent with knees squeezed tighter than anyone else. Hundreds of other Kentucky children were hunkered down too, fighting for their lives at the same time, during what would later be called the Super Tornado Outbreak of 1974. Evidently the Hail Marys worked for us because Owensboro made it through the deadly tornadoes with only power outages.

While our city was spared from the funnels that April day, nearby towns, especially Brandenburg, KY was devastated. In total, the storm claimed 330 lives, many of them children. The super outbreak of tornadoes was the second worst storm of the century. The National Weather Service even detected a noticeable rise and fall of the Ohio River as water was displaced. A river tsunami was not one of my fears at the time, but maybe should have been.

Tornadoes continued to terrify me and unfortunately, they weren't done with Owensboro yet. It was a good thing I vowed to remember from age four forward. If it weren't for the combine in the cornfield which triggered my youthful memory, I might have forgotten Aunt Mary's farm altogether by the year 2000- the farm in which a future tornado was already making plans to blow away.

I would have forgotten about Aunt Mary's chicken coop if I hadn't seared it in my memory. I might have forgotten about the time Aunt Mary brought a cardboard box of baby chicks for my cousin, Pam, and I to play with on her kitchen floor. The saying, "Don't count your chickens before they hatch" should be amended, for there was no use counting them afterwards either. When we released the chicks on the linoleum floor, the fur balls with feet dispersed in every direction, like a handful of tossed jacks. Naming them didn't help. I'm not sure all the chicks made it back in the box on our watch.

It would have been a shame to forget Aunt Mary's homemade ice cream that we worked so hard for-the kind with rock salt and a crank to turn. Our aunt called it custard, but it tasted like ice cream to us. And the outhouse, I wouldn't want to forget about our sanctuary. When vicious dogs down the lane chased us, we threw our bikes down in the gravel and took off running to the nearest shelter, the outhouse.

Stray cats abounded at Aunt Mary's, as did the pigs in the pen. We'd grab a handful of corn from the silo and throw it to the pigs, before jumping in the pen with them. It was like a playground, with pigs and a pond in the middle, every child's dreamland. Abandoned cars without wheels rested in the same field. We snuck up to the doorless vehicles and tried not to rouse the giant pig inside. Boy, did she squeal.

I remembered the cattails, the kissing gate, the apricot tree, sleeping under the stars, a peacock's screech, the porch glider covered in quilts, the massive pear tree, the scary cellar on the outside of the house. I would be glad someday that I took mental inventory of the farm. I would not want my last memories of Aunt Mary's place reduced to rubble.

It would all be gone when the 2000 tornado stripped the land. A gaping hole in the cellar would expose the canned green beans and distilled water. The cellar's contents, a concrete shelter, parts of a stairway, foundational logs, and a wardrobe were the only things the tornado left behind. Oh…and a wooden leg. Aunt Mary survived the Owensboro tornado which destroyed her home, but then she was left homeless. "Gone," was all she would say. And if I had not committed the farm to memory, my childhood past too would be gone, as in gone with the wind.

10

IF THE SHOE FITS

My grandmother owned a liquor store and was a shoes-aholic. I grew up in that same liquor store and have a shoe aversion. Based on this logic, I concluded that environment combined with heredity does not necessarily predispose you to certain things, be it alcoholism or shoe obsession. I was living proof.

Grandmother inherited her shoe fetish from the get-go. Her father, my great grandfather, Peter Charles Gropp partnered with his brother in ownership of the Gropp Brothers Shoe Store on Owensboro's Main Street. In 1905, a store advertisement read: "The only exclusive shoe store in the city selling high class shoes." The shoe store was in business the same time as the Murphy Chair Company, Woolworths and the Rudd House Hotel.

I wonder if all those high class customers knew my grandmother sometimes slipped on a pair of those high heeled shoes for just a little while before sneaking them back into the box to sell. She couldn't help herself with so many shoes and only two feet. No high heel was high enough.

Back then, the Gropp family lived in a mansion on Griffith Avenue. Another news article stated that the house was purchased with inheritance money. My Aunt Hazel was mortified. As the oldest of the Gropp children, she pleaded with her shoe salesman father, "How humiliating! What possessed you to tell that to the newspaper? (Or something along those lines).

My great grandfather said, "We don't want people to think I make that much money selling shoes."

When he died an untimely death, Great Grandfather left our Granny Gropp a widow with young children. My grandmother was only twelve at the time of her father's death, and had to move from the Griffith mansion to a rental home. All the Gropp children managed to at least have shoes on their feet.

When my grandmother was in her nineties, she paid a visit to her childhood home on Griffith. I asked her if it was still familiar and she said, "Every nook and cranny." When the home belonged to the Gropps, the land stretched from Griffith to Ford Avenue. Sometimes Grandmother drove past her old Kentucky home with me in the car. She drove slowly past the sweeping lawn with unseen gardens that were now locked away from her. The closest building to the road was the cheese house. Its round thatched roof reminded me of Medieval Times. To Grandmother, it reminded her of the good ol' days.

My grandmother's love for shoes continued past her

father's death. She accumulated many pairs and collected them like a dryer vent collects lint. But the shoe love affair was either stunted or skipped generations when my grandmother had four sons. I came along as the first granddaughter, the long awaited girl my grandmother wished to share her shoes with.

My dad called from the hospital to tell his mother she was the new grandmother of a baby girl. Grandmother left him hanging. Dad had the phone receiver in one hand and a dial tone in one ear. My grandmother hung up on her son, proud dad and all. She called the hospital herself to ensure that a baby girl was not a hoax. "Can you tell me what the Van Meter baby is?" She would only believe "It's a girl!" from the doctor's staff which had been in the delivery room. From then on, Grandmother squeezed me and said, "I love you so much that it hurts me."

I could barely breathe from the bear hug and answered truthfully, "It hurts me too."

My grandmother and I shared many experiences, but a love of shoes was not one of them. My sister inherited that gene. I on the other hand, inherited the "Jean," that was my grandmother's nickname for my first name. I was called by my full name of Jean Michelle when I was ornery. Grandmother was called "Mean Jean" when she was spry and feisty.

Grandmother often took me on an errand to Rain's Shoe Hospital, an urgent care facility for shoes on Frederica Street. Grandmother loved shoes so much that she would rather take them to the doctor than go to the doctor herself. Through her, I realized how strongly people felt about shoes to the point of first aid. Even in the Cinderella fairytale, it all came down to the shoe in the end. You either have the shoe gene or you don't.

Shoe love was in my DNA, but the wires got crossed and I inherited a shoe loathing. Grandmother often bought me Madame Alexander dolls from Kuester's but the first thing I would lose would be their shoes. I went barefooted myself most of the time and was the brunt of many Kentucky jokes even as an adult. Shoe shopping was pure torture for me, almost as bad as antique shopping. Because of my narrow heel, I wore corrective shoes until I was old enough to know my shoes were different from everyone else's. I wanted the Buster Brown shoes my brother wore, or at least close replicas. I begged to have the Red Goose shoes most of all. They came with a special prize, a plastic golden egg filled with worthless trinkets.

While Downtown in the children's shoe store, I longingly watched other children receive their reward from the red goose. Golden eggs rolled into their stubby waiting hands. The prizes weren't any good, but the happy children clutched the eggs tightly, almost forgetting the new shoes.

I was deprived of shopping for prize-winning shoes but recently searched the EBay website for a Red Goose machine to see if one really existed, and not just in my bad dreams. Unbelievably, one was available for $650. Apparently money cannot buy happiness, but it can still buy shoes.

Today, new shoeboxes remind me of my grandmother who has now gone to Heaven. The boxes suggest I have big shoes to fill. Once while sorting through boxes in Grandmother's otherwise empty house, I came upon a little black book. The battered book was well-worn with its spine barely intact and a rubber band holding the pages together. My name was listed several times in that little black prayer book of Grandmother's. Perhaps the only thing which kept my heart from evil while growing up was the grace of God and the fact I had a praying grandmother. I miss her so much that it hurts me.

11

WHERE EVERYBODY KNOWS YOUR NAME

"Forgive us our trespasses..." I couldn't remember the rest. The Lord's Prayer was on the tip of my Bonnie Bell, strawberry flavored lips. I recited the prayer every night and couldn't believe it would leave me now when I needed it the most. I lifted my eyes towards my teacher, but I only saw my own distorted reflection in Sister Mary Clemet's bifocals.

Sister moved to the next victim, but I wasn't out of the doghouse yet. Hopefully this would be my last stand. Those of us left standing by our desks were a stiff regiment of third graders. Our knees knocked together but that could have been from the frigid room temperature. The school board required the heat to be set on 65 degrees to save money during the cold snap. I longed for the radiator's hiss so my blood could reach my numbed toes. Besides, Sister needed to warm up too or get the bee out of her habit.

Teachers came with different expectations, with the nuns tending to be stricter. Owensboro's very first teacher was a drifter. They called her Aunt Sukey because she was so loving and well-liked. Before arriving in Owensboro, she boarded a steamship bound for Cloverport, but the ship sank. Aunt Sukey drifted to the Big O by hanging onto a piece of wreckage. She decided to go with the flow and remain in Owensboro to teach.

I was no closer to thawing out when I dared to look at my classmates. Those who were lucky enough to recite their Catechism correctly were sitting down, staring at the dummies still standing. One peer mouthed to me, "As we forgive those who trespass against us." Yes, I knew it. I just panicked and forgot what I remembered.

Sister momentarily forgot about those standing too. Another classmate was singled out when she yanked him by the bangs and did that special whisper that was really a holler. "When you gonna cut this hair, Mister?" Alas, he kept cutting it, but it kept growing. It was one of the usual bowl haircuts that boys his age had either that or an afro.

I was anxious for class to change and to return to Mrs. Todd's homeroom. She gave her students a picture of herself for Christmas. The boys in class openly admitted their crushes for Mrs. Todd and were especially proud. Since wallet pictures were in limited supply, usually eight of them, the miniature photos were reserved for special people. I still have my wallet-sized photo of Mrs. Todd.

The smashed noses against the classroom door's pane meant the other class was waiting in the hall for class to change. Our class was ending too and students jumped up to line up. Since I was already up, I was second in line to leave the lion's den. In this class, I could see where waterboarding and Baptism could be confused.

Just when I thought the inquest was over, I jumped when I heard Sister rattle off several names, mine included. "Michelle, you will stand by your desk tomorrow too." I tiptoed out of the den but the lion wasn't going to sleep tonight. Boy, I wished she didn't know my name.

The door burst open and the inmates were free at last. Our conga line snaked then suddenly swerved to the side. All twenty of us safely sidestepped a puddle of puke in the hallway as the janitor hastily poured orange saw dust on it. We were used to it and never lost our appetites, especially on Friday when the cafeteria served rectangle pizzas with a cardboard pint of milk. It turned out that the sausage on the pizza was really soybeans. They went to a lot of trouble to make it look and feel like meat. This was back when ketchup was considered a vegetable.

Report cards were handed out on the last day of class. I knew my social studies grade would be superior since I had memorized all the state capitals. I could recite all fifty capitals but could not remember the last verse of the Lord's Prayer. The front of the report card revealed whether you were promoted to the next grade or not. I snuck a look around the class to see if any faces looked shocked in case someone had flunked.

When I opened the report card, the A's and B's caught my eye. Then one C glared back at me. I traced my shaky finger along the chart, certain the bad grade was in religion. But no, the category was a write-in, handwritten with a different pen belonging to the art teacher. I got a C in art! My future as an artist was crushed. In third grade, I drew a pretty good turtle. Forty years later, I still drew a pretty good turtle. My artistic talent stagnated in third grade, not even crawling at a turtle's pace.

Nothing kept pace with summer vacation. It flew by, but not without us eeking every ounce of playtime from every day. Even with my Cinderella wind-up watch, I missed curfew. Everyone else had a curfew of 'dark' and ran like a bat when the street lights blinked on. But my curfew was based on the clock's face. I was confused with all the quarter 'tils and quarter afters and stayed in trouble until digital clocks became mainstream. Untied shoelaces posed an issue for me as well. Had Velcro been around, I would not have spent my summers barefooted. Then again, I was from Kentucky.

The sticky heat made you think that summer days would never go away. The ice cream man's magic jingle bells were magic to our neighborhood gang's ears. Our appetites were only limited by lack of funds. We passed on the twenty-five cent drumsticks and rocket pops, but could afford the three-cent, tube-shaped bubblegum if we pooled our money together. We got a lot of bang for our cents because the gum was frozen and took the Jaws of Life to make it chewable.

We worked as a team while one kid hailed the ice cream man and the rest scurried for pennies, as fast as their dirty bare feet could go. Once, I was the designated kid left to stall the ice cream man. It was the day that Mom told me that if I came in the house one more time and let in any more flies, I would have to stay inside and dust the top of the refrigerator.

I chose to talk to a stranger instead. He all but said, "Do you want some candy?" The ice cream man asked my name. I told him, Michelle. He asked how old I was.

Then my friend, Lenny came running with pennies. The ice cream man handed me the bubblegum to distribute and the transaction was over. We went back to the games kids play.

The following Saturday I watched my usual cartoons of Josie and the Pussycats and Speed Buggy. Captain Kangaroo with Mr. Green Jeans was my favorite, but it was a weekday series, along with Underdog. After cartoons, I planned to capture Casey Kasem's 100 song countdown on my tape recorder if my recycled cassette tapes didn't require rewinding with a pencil.

Cartoons were interrupted by the ringing telephone. I waited for someone else to answer it and then finally skipped over the beanbag chair to catch the phone before it stopped ringing. I answered it with an out-of-breath, "Hello!"

My greeting was met with silence and I almost hung up before a voice just as breathless whispered, "Michelle" on the other end.

"Who is this? I mean who, may I ask is calling?" I changed my tune with a more polite question even though I didn't mean it.

"Guess."

"Um, Uncle Bob?"

"Yes, that's right."

"Well, Dad's not home." I just wanted to watch my show. I dragged the everlasting phone cord into the TV room in time to hear the end of the Oscar Mayer Weiner commercial, b-o-l-o-g-n-a. I had to stay tuned to see what would happen next week on my shows.

The caller continued, "We can just talk."

Oh brother, this was Saturday and I had things to do like fix the twisted Slinky or watch my brother dig a hole to China with GI Joe driving the Tonka dump truck. But

I was polite and said, "Yes sir," at appropriate times, because the saying seemed to appease adults. I listened with one ear and tuned in to the TV with the other. 'Uncle Bob' caught my attention when he proceeded to tell me where my body parts were on my almost fourth-grade body.

I left the phone cord dangling and went in search of Mom. Uncle Bob gave me the creeps. By the time I found an adult, the phone beeped repeatedly, a reminder to hang up because the line was dead. Dad told me later that Uncle Bob never called.

"But he said it was him."

I persisted and felt like I was in trouble for lying. Dad asked what the caller said but I was too uncomfortable to mention the stupid stuff, something about pumpkins. With a worried look, Dad told me not to answer the phone anymore. In those days, we were trained like Pavlov's dogs to respond to bells. If a phone rang, you answered it; if ice cream bells sounded, you ran for loose change. So on the next Saturday when it was just me and the TV again, I again answered the persistent phone.

"Michelle...this is Uncle Bob."

I gently replaced the receiver so perhaps the caller wouldn't realize I had hung up on him. It was rude to hang up on an adult and I could get in big trouble. I would just say I forgot I wasn't supposed to answer the phone, and had to hang up. I never told Dad that Uncle Bob called back that day, or the next, or the next.

I knew it wasn't really Uncle Bob, but I didn't know who else to call the voice at the other end, just a nameless dread. The calls were so frequent that the caller had me at "Michelle." When he whispered my name, I'd hang up instantly. I wished he didn't know my name. I hated the way he said it.

There was my answer. I would change my name. My dad called me "Shell Bell." I could use a nickname and everyone who knew me could use it too. Strangers would still call me Michelle, which included 'Uncle Bob.' Such was my process of elimination and I hoped 'Uncle Bob' wasn't smarter than a fourth grader. Everything was about to change, including my name. "Goodbye Michelle, my trusted friend. We knew each other until we were nine or ten." I just wanted to be a normal kid again.

The fear of strangers was added to my bucket list of frightening encounters. Strangers were right up there with tornadoes. In a flash, my last religion class came rushing back to me. I remembered the rest: Deliver us from evil. Amen.

12

MICHELLE REMEMBERS

To be a friend, you had to draw blood. As blood sisters, my neighbor and I pricked our fingers with a needle and rubbed bloody pinkies together to represent sisterhood. I wanted to be a good friend, but I hated blood and anything which pricked my fingers, especially splinters. If Dad saw a splinter, he would say, "Get me the tweezers," as he reached for his Zippo lighter. A measly fragment embedded in the skin was preferable to passing over hot coals and being plucked out.

We couldn't help splinters, but becoming blood buddies was self-inflicted pain. We had other means as well. Our worst idea was the 'tie one end of string to the doorknob and the other end to the loose tooth' scheme. What we'd do for a quarter from the tooth fairy! The

CIA would be sanctioned for engaging in these torture methods for terrorists.

Despite the pains of friendship, we had joy and we had fun. Seasons in the Sun became my theme song. Every time Terry Jacks sang, "Goodbye Michelle my little one," I squeezed some tears. But goodbye Michelle it had to be. Change was the name of the game for fourth grade. I became a number instead of a name. According to the Pringles can mail boxes, I was number nineteen in my fourth grade class. All tests and written grades were distributed through the chip canisters. I only reminded the teacher seven times that first day that my new name was Shelly. It was easier to refer to me as number nineteen.

Johnny was number twenty. He was the new kid from Indiana and we thought he was a hunk. A hunk was meant to be a good thing. Girls swarmed around him that first day me included. We confiscated his phone number and pursued him for months, maybe even years. I still remember that number-lessons learned from a stalker, I guess. Not in my wildest dreams could I imagine that someday in the future, I would sing in his sister's wedding where I would meet my own husband. There was a greater purpose for my stalking him.

After that first day of fourth grade, I told Johnny to call me Shelly. "That's not her name," my friends said and made the cuckoo sign that I was crazy.

"Oh yes it is. From now on, I'm Shelly."

Lenny called me Shelly Belly and I heard a Smelly Shelly too.

"I don't care. Just don't call me Michelle."

Soon, only one person called me Michelle. It was the voice on the phone that hissed when he said it. I hung up on the hiss and willed him out of my mind. I had bigger fish to fry in fourth grade.

Most of life's lessons occurred while walking home from school. We were enlightened while on the playground, and at church, but the real learning took place after the teachers let the monkeys out. The most fertile battleground was the soil between the elementary school and the neighborhood where our group walked as a travelling mosh pit, slowly dwindling until the one who lived farthest trudged alone.

The dirt mounds on the way were for King of the Hill. The king was a bully who pushed everyone down the hill. It didn't get any more brutal than that. Unfortunately, over the hill was the only way home. Once on the way, my friend Lenny sunk in mud up to his knees. The rest of us ran to tell his mother he had been swallowed in quicksand. She didn't believe us and took her time. By the time we got back to Lenny, he was then up to his waist in mud.

I had bad dreams about my friend swallowed by a sinkhole for years. I almost lost him underneath King of the Hill. Lenny survived the mudslide and made it to our regularly scheduled picnic at the sewer on Saturday. A drainage ditch at the end of our street was where neighbor kids spent time feasting on its banks and crawling inside the drain. Peanut butter and pickle on saltines was the perfect picnic fare for a sewer.

While walking home from the sewer, (most of my life was spent walking) the older kids rambled on, talking smack. Suddenly, my face stung and I stumbled backwards. Tears pooled in my eyes as I stared through the blur at the older girl who had smacked me. Everyone else stared at the handprint on my face.

"Why did you do that for?" Lenny charged the girl.

"Because she flipped me off," she said, pointing to me.

Stunned, I mustered a pitiful, "What?"

"You gave me the finger!" she accused. I looked down at my hands. What was she talking about?

The older girl flipped me off, proud to illustrate what she thought I did. I didn't respond because I didn't know I was supposed to be insulted. She jeered, "You really don't know. It's because you're so green."

That was when she took it upon herself to inform me how babies were made. At the time, I worried about my training bra straps showing through my white uniform blouse and was anxious about shaving my legs for the first time. I was obsessed with Love's Baby Soft perfume and just started using Gee Your Hair Smells Terrific shampoo because it really did smell terrific. As if puberty didn't pose enough change, I had to change my name, ward off a stalker, and now, be burdened with the birds and the bees. To top it off, teachers warned that the Metric System would soon take over the world. If we didn't learn it, we would be left behind. Millimeters made me nervous. Teachers would know the feeling when their encyclopedias were left behind.

Fourth grade seemed to be the most dangerous place on the planet. Thank goodness my name was written in my grandmother's little black prayer book. I should have reminded her to update my name change in it. If I learned anything in fourth grade, it was how good it was to be green. I straddled the fence between playing with my Easy Bake Oven and chasing boys while actually enjoying it. This weird dichotomy continued that following summer. It took the whole neighborhood to arrange my first kiss during summer vacation. I did not have a say-so in the matter. The gang decided the where, the when, and even the who. They would choose the older boy with the braces.

The twelve-year old boy had a Hefty bicycle for paper routes. He motioned to me while patting the handlebars, indicating I was to ride on top of the basket where newspapers were usually kept. As he steered us to our kissing destination of Shively Park, I thought we would kiss in the baseball dugouts, but no, we passed the merry-go-round, swings, and monkey bars too, all of which still secretly appealed to me. He rode out of the park and nearly wrecked while plowing his bike into the nearby cornfield. I fought to land on my feet after being thrown from the handlebars.

There I sat among the ears of corn and endured my first kiss. I waited for it to be over and was as polite as possible when asking, "Can we go now?" We sealed the end of our relationship with one kiss. Not a word was spoken to each other again. I felt dirty, probably because I was. I had mud all over me from the corn field. But I was a big girl now. I brushed the dust off, hopped back on the handlebars, and acted as if nothing ever happened. The gang wanted to hear all the gory details, but I didn't want to talk about it. There was nothing to talk about, really.

That next week while playing outside with neighbors, the familiar jingle of the ice cream man teased our ears. Kids bolted in search of money. It was my turn again to stall the ice cream man, so I stayed to intercept the treats until my friends could cough up enough coins for frozen bubblegum. I stood on the curb by myself. The ice cream man pulled up next to me. The music stopped. He was in no hurry as he crossed his arms and stared at my legs. My feet fidgeted on the hot pavement while he watched. An uncomfortable charge in the air made me stop dancing. Then he slowly smiled and hissed, "Michelle."

13

GROWING PAINS

Finding out that 'Uncle Bob' was the ice cream man was par for the year. Michelle was long gone and I adopted a new motto. "When the going gets tough, the tough get going." Second only to the bridge jump/follow the crowd narrative my dad was famous for this one-liner. Couple the clause with most physical ailments my mother summed up as 'growing pains,' and I was the typical misunderstood teenager. There was no use complaining, only to hear horror stories of my parents walking miles to school in the snow, barefooted and all that. Even that was not an option for me. Once I wore shorts in the middle of winter and Dad grounded me from everything fun.

"How long am I grounded?" I asked.
"Until you get some common sense," he said.
"Um, how long is that?"

This last question was used against me in the family court of law. I was grounded another time when the kitchen caught on fire. Like a good babysitter, I attempted to provide supper for my siblings, baked potatoes for all. The microwave was set to seven minutes so each potato would be good and done. Instead of wasting time waiting, I went off to play records in my room, playing Rhinestone Cowboy, my sister, Lesley's favorite. We sang together until our brother Michael banged on the door yelling, "Fire!"

I casually walked down the hall until I saw smoke billowing from the living room's shuttered doors. He was right. It appeared the whole house was on fire, although the flames were contained in the kitchen microwave. Back then, microwaves were as large as refrigerators and took up an entire corner of the kitchen.

A gallon of Kool-Aid sat on the counter, so I dumped purple sugar water on the fire. It worked, although the microwave was still smoldering when my parents came home. The fiery drama inspired them to hire Cindy, a real babysitter. All was again well, but the game of Hot Potato hasn't appealed to me since.

The traumas of the teenage years have been dulled by time, although the memories remain. Most tough lessons weren't so bad really. At the time though, the situations could make or break the fragile adolescent psyche.

I lived a blessed life in Owensboro during the seventies and eighties, but it was not always so simple as shag carpets and shag haircuts, although we even carpeted used cable spools in the shag. The newfangled shag tables were a novelty item. As it turned out, there was more to life than worshipping the sun, anointing myself with Hawaiian Tropic oil, Donny Osmond's

Puppy Love, Channel No 5, and real dyed Easter eggs. Not everything was as orderly as I once believed, after they started making test tube babies. Some topics weren't even to be found in the Encyclopedia Britannica like Ayatollah, which I needed for Mrs. Mountain's special report in seventh grade.

However, I had ample time to research the Shah of Iran with the extended days in Mr. Newton's class. If one student talked out of turn, the whole class stayed after school as punishment. Holding an entire classroom hostage was a teacher's opportunity for spring cleaning with free labor. The enslaved did come with attitudes though, hardly worth the work.

Mr. Newton blanketed our collective punishment in a lesson: "The rain falls on the good and the bad." That meant that all paid the price for one person's misconduct. We caught on quickly to teacher rhetoric. When we realized halfway through the school day that we would all be held liable, we spent the rest of the afternoon seizing the day by earning the punishment, each in our own way.

After one week of 'doing time' after school, a classroom mutiny was brewing. It was Julie's turn to dust-mop the floor that day. When Mr. Newton stepped out of the room, students mocked, "The rain falls on the good and the bad," over and over. Julie got caught up in our murmuring and marched her dirty mop to the front of the room and shook it vigorously over the top of Mr. Newton's desk. We all roared. So she did it again. I'll never forget the scene as the afternoon sun shone through the tinted school windows and emphasized the dusty desk. The filtered sunlight suspended all the dust particles in slow motion as they floated around Julie and her mop. The scene reminded me of church with the stained glass prisms highlighting an altar and Saint Julie with a dusty halo over her head.

That was when Mr. Newton stopped short at the classroom door and saw what was happening to his immaculate throne. Julie didn't see him and kept right on shaking. She always blushed when she laughed and was having a really good time with it too. Her delighted face was in stark contrast to the teacher's smirk as he leaned against the door frame with arms crossed and fists balled up.

With wide eyes, we tried to warn Julie, but it was too late. Our class stayed after school for another solid week. Lesson Learned. This time it was worth it. We had encouraged Julie, and in fact, wished we had done it ourselves. It was our dust too. The rain really did fall on the good and the bad. And sometimes dust bunnies fell on the teacher's lesson plans.

When I didn't have an entire classroom to back me up, I learned to cope by spending time in the liquor store. I gave out the phone number to my grandparent's liquor store in case my friends needed to reach me: 684-1635. The environment did not contribute to any delinquency on my part, but instead, was where many of my life lessons took place. The Dugout liquor store was a cherished childhood memory.

My grandmother and papa owned the Dugout, a deli and package store at the junction on East Ninth, right across the street from the A & P grocery store and the G.E. plant. General Electric was already on the national radar for its vacuum radio tubes and the light bulbs which illuminated the first night game in Major League Baseball between the Reds and the Phillies in 1935.

Ronald Reagan once visited Owensboro's prestigious plant before becoming President of the United States. Reagan may have also visited the Dugout while in town. The Dugout featured curbside corndogs called 'Quickies' and the famous Bullburger from its deli. When G.E.'s 8000 female shift workers traipsed across the street for Bullburgers and Quickies for lunch each day, the Dugout was the place to be.

The Dugout was the first in town to offer this curbside service, food straight from its corner lot. Another of Papa's innovative ideas was even quicker to spread-the Dugout's drive-thru liquor store, another first for Owensboro. Papa was a smart entrepreneur, a term which hadn't been coined yet. He was a man before his time. (See Bullburger recipe at end of chapter)

The Joe Ford Museum, which housed snakes and a planetarium, was my old stomping ground, just down the road from the Dugout. The building had been a library, a museum, and later an art gallery. Before these, the spot was a buffalo stomping ground. Real buffalos roamed before any of us travelled Frederica Street, an early buffalo thoroughfare extending from a salt lick at Panther Creek to the Ohio River. The buffalo trail was transformed into a mule trail when 'mulecars' of townspeople rode in carriages pulled by mules through the city streets. On the day that a brass band led the first mulecar Downtown with flags and banners, over six hundred people paid a nickel for a ride. By the 1920s, the trail became a rail when ten electric streetcars roamed Frederica on eight miles of tracks. Modern cities boasted of rails-to-trails, but Owensboro had trails-to-rails as old buffalo grounds were transformed into streetcar lanes.

As a child, I worked the Dugout liquor store grounds

by picking up cigarette butts from the parking lot. I did not complain, did not wear gloves, and did not use hand sanitizer before I held my grubby hands out to collect twenty-five dollars for cleaning up the litter. I was still convinced that littering was a felony crime and the settlement money I earned could purchase more Mallo Cups, Pixie Stix straws, and candy cigarettes at the Quick Pick gas station next door.

Because I was a candy junkie, I frequented the dentist, also across the street from the Dugout. Between my thirteen mercury-filled cavities and some pulled teeth, I often cleaned up litter with a mouthful of cotton gauze until the Novocain's numbness wore off. As soon as it did, I safely removed the cotton to suck on more candy.

Some Dugout customers passed on the liquor and formed a line behind the cigarette machine in the middle of the store. I was always pleased to see the line. Because of their smoking habit, I had job security. The machine was like a giant slot machine with over twenty pull tabs for different cigarette brands. I pulled a tab every time I walked past and sometimes a packet would drop in the slot. Too bad it wasn't candy.

Part of my job involved dusting the liquor bottles, with special diligence given to the Crown Royal and Captain Morgan novelty editions. I also dusted the table shaped like a Martini glass with a stuffed olive between its table legs. The wine cellar was the prettiest with wood panel walls and fake grapes hanging over the doorway, but I wasn't allowed to dust those old bottles. They stayed dusty, but valuable. After finishing odd jobs, I slipped into the employee snack room where Ina shared her potato salad made from scratch. For years, I thought Ina was family, at least a distant aunt. She was a fixture in the store since I could remember and her shared recipes were in our index file marked 'Family Recipes.'

My work breaks were taken behind the mammoth cash register, while I spun in circles on the rotating stool. One button opened the cash drawer, where I arranged all the twenties, tens, and fives. Underneath the cashbox were larger bills which always gave me a jolt, especially the ones with Ben Franklin's picture. Just one push of a button and money was at your fingertips. The Dugout had been robbed before, but never while I was there.

Customers entered from the busy street, through a glass door which rang like a doorbell when opened. I passed time by watching the traffic and inking the stamp used for hand-stamping dates on every sales receipt. Next, I wetted the yellow sponge used for postage stamps. Back then, you either licked stamps to make them stick or pressed them into a fancy yellow sponge.

Papa joined me during this downtime, with stories about my dad when he was my age. Dad's nickname of "Buzz" was derived from the buzz bomb, Germany's V-1 flying bomb dreaded by the Allies. Dad lucked out though; another name for the same bomb was doodlebug. He never could shake the Buzz nickname, which told me he had earned it and tales were bound to surface.

Papa didn't know the half of it though, like the times when Dad took a ride in the seat carriage across the bear trap's roaring water, flowing through the old lock and dam on the river. There he fished off the middle of the dam until catching enough fish to give away to the folks who lived by the river. On the way home, he rode his bike, stopping through 'colored town' where mothers came to the street to relieve him of his catch. He had to get rid of the fish before booking it home to play in his afternoon baseball game, for he did have his priorities in order. After all, it was 1958 – the year his Babe Ruth Baseball team vied for the World Series championship. Dad's chance to wear jersey #14 in Vancouver, British Columbia during their sesquicentennial celebration trumped fishing from Lock and Dam #46 on Owensboro's Ohio River.

Babe Ruth baseball was a big deal to the town. Dad still tells his own stories about his All-star team and remembers specific details as if they happened yesterday, like playing left field and batting ninth. He recalls all of his teammates, along with Coach Ernie Knight, who was in his early twenties at the time, and not much older than the boys he coached. Lloyd Nash, the assistant coach, was teammate Ricky's brother, who was the same age as the boys on the team.

During the Ohio Valley Regional Game, right before the World Series tournament, Owensboro was losing in mid-innings. Dad was up to bat with runners on base. Coaching third base coach, Coach Ernie called a time-out to give Dad a 'pep talk' which went like this: "If you don't get a hit, you won't start the next game." Dad would not have told this story unless he had delivered a double which knocked in a couple of runs and sparked their team to victory. The hit was actually a grounder which went under the temporary picket fence, but that was good enough, still out of the park.

Dad must have gotten into additional mischief along the railroad tracks next to his childhood home because he was extra strict with me when it came to tracks. The most I ever did was deface pennies on the tracks, which I suppose was a federal crime. But I never hopped a slow moving train which took me across town. Dad claimed it was his brother who did that and not him.

Papa told me other stories of when my mom and dad went steady, as they called it. I saw where Dad got his round-about narrations because Papa also spoke in parables. I waited for Papa to mention bridge jumping too, but he didn't. Instead, he told me of a conversation when Dad was a teenager. "Son, did I ever tell you about the farmer who liked green beans?" Even if Dad recalled the story, Papa would preach it again. It saved more time to say he'd never heard it before. Papa launched into the retelling of the tale:

"There was once a farmer who loved green beans and only ate green beans. Because he only tried one thing, that's all he knew. It's a wonder he didn't get tired of green beans. Just imagine- never tasting tomatoes or squash, never enjoying corn or potatoes. All he cared about was green beans. Green beans forever."

Papa likened the green beans allegory to my dad going steady with my mom. "Son, what conclusion can you make from the story?"

Dad said, "I don't know, but I sure like green beans!"

I still laugh to think that Dad can't stand cucumbers. Well, the farmer ended up marrying green beans, and together they had me, their first child. Going on fifty years of marriage now, Mom and Dad were serious about the green beans forever part. Technically, that was Dad's life lesson, not mine. Papa reserved special anecdotes for me, like the time I didn't make cheerleading. My cheerleading career may not have amounted to a hill of beans, but at the time cheerleading was my life.

From the Pop Warner stage, young girls were primed to tryout in public for a cheerleading team. The Cardinals squad was the coveted, elite team for up and coming cheerleaders. In order to make the Cardinal's, schmoozing the coach, performing a back handspring flip, and pointed toes splits were required. Competition was fierce. If Tonya Harding had lived in town then, she would have been a Cardinal.

Contestants performed cheers in front of a biased audience and a row of judges. Each cheer began with a holler, "Ready? Okay!" You asked the question and you answered it too. Those who made the team were announced publicly, with their squeals joining the jumping huddle of fellow cheerleaders. The other ninety girls were left on the bench until their parents picked them up.

During one try-out for the Immaculate Tigers, I was

left on the bench. My parents had even enlisted me in gymnastic lessons at Joy's Dance Studio. After months of almost breaking my neck and an entire summer of stretching my groin to do the splits, I learned a stunt or two. Proud of my physical achievements, I taught another peer everything my parents had paid for. I freely shared my new expertise and gave her confidence that she, too should go out for cheerleading team.

There we both were at tryouts with individual numbers safety-pinned to our chests. When the judging was done, her number was called and mine was not. I sat the bench waiting for Papa to pick me up so I could cry alone. Some girls wailed in front of everyone, but I was saving my tears, at least for the ride home.

I threw my useless pom-poms in the backseat and climbed in Papa's car. He let the silence speak several minutes before finally speaking, "It is better not to make the team while everyone believes you should have than to make the team and everyone believe you shouldn't have." He was not referring to my friend who made the team, but spoke in generalities.

I wanted to skip school the next day instead of facing the humiliation of being a former cheerleader, but faking a fever was a dangerous game. On one hand, you might be given the little pink 'baby aspirin,' we called it, but on the other hand, or rather, end, you could get stuck with a thermometer. Our thermometers didn't beep when done; they stayed in place a long time. I couldn't chance it, so I chose to go to school.

Papa's words of wisdom did not sink in until I got to school. As I walked to class, friends huddled around to tell me what a good job I did at try-outs and that I should have made the team. My tears from the night before were replaced with smiles as I was genuinely happy for the compliments and 'get well soon' wishes. Not all the girls who made the cheer team were as happy as I was. Some weren't congratulated by anyone other than me. During Mr. Thompson's math class, I saw a tear trickle down one cheerleader's face. Papa was right.

He was clairvoyant too. Some weeks later, nurses visited our school. We frequently had head lice checks in the lunchroom foyer so I thought this was another one of those. Instead, the nurses instructed each girl to lean forward with hands clasped as if diving, while they traced a line up our spines. Afterward, I received a letter to take home to my parents. The letter indicated I had scoliosis, a curvature of the spine.

I had never heard of scoliosis before, but anything ending in "osis" sounded like a contagious disease involving sneezing. I was devastated with the diagnosis and felt like the hunchback of Daviess County after I read Deenie, a book about a girl with the same "osis" whose character wore a monstrous back brace to correct her curve.

An x-ray revealed the extent of the s-curve in my lumbar spine. A protractor like one used in geometry measured the curve degree. The doctor's face was grim while he added each angle, indicating my crooked spine was askew by nineteen degrees. At twenty degrees, a back brace was prescribed-the dreaded, rigid cast no one could autograph. I was one degree away and still growing. Therefore, my vertebrae were still moving. As if given a cancer diagnosis, I did not save any tears for later, but wailed in the doctor's office chair.

The doctor gave me a one month reprieve for my spine to adjust, but warned me to brace myself for the brace. In that window of time, I stretched my body to its limits while in physical therapy, but was still told not get my hopes up. I was advised against bearing children in the future. My mother openly cried at this verdict. To me, childbirth was worlds away compared to the dire near future of wearing maternity clothes a size too big to fit over a bulky brace when you weren't pregnant. Mother and I shed tears for different reasons.

Evidently, scoliosis really was related to growing pains. My body grew too fast. By seventh grade, I was heads taller than most of the class except for Julie. Cheerleading was also a factor in the spinal curve. As a tall 'base,' I held other girls on my back and shoulders for cheerleading pyramids. Since I did not make the latest team, my back actually took a break in a good way.

During my trial month, I followed an exercise regimen stiffer than the therapists recommended, and multiplied the exercise routines before facing the brace from hell. A wooden board was inserted between my mattresses and I became an exercising machine. Others thought I was 'stuck up' because my posture was so rigid. I walked as if I wore an invisible brace anyway. Mom even stopped saying, "Keep your shoulders back." When I thought about the brace, I pounded my fists on the floor and straightened up for more push-ups.

I was obsessed with scoliosis and cried a lot in my room behind a closed door. On one of those bad days, I slumped against my dresser and noticed my puffy eyes, swollen from tears, in the mirror tray on top. The rest of the tray was covered with other faces I didn't recognize. Every time Dad went to a funeral, he brought home a holy card and dropped it in the tray. Each card depicted a picture of a saint, had a prayer on the back, and read

"In memory of..." on the bottom. I had a good collection of them, almost a full deck of holy cards. I wasn't sure what to do with them, but was afraid to throw them away.

I flipped one of the cards over and read the prayer. I was good at memorizing prayers by then and wrote this one on my heart:

God hath not promised skies always blue,
Flower-strewn pathways all our lives through;
God hath not promised sun without rain,
Joy without sorrow, or peace without pain.
But God hath promised strength for the day,
Rest for the labor and light for the way,
Grace for the trials, help from above,
Unfailing sympathy and undying love.
(Words by Annie J. Flint, 1919)

I committed the words to memory and resumed the push-up position again. I don't know whether it was physical, emotional, or spiritual exhaustion, but I fell face-down on the blue carpet and could go no more. So I prayed. For the first time ever, I prayed by myself, for myself, with no one prompting me. I don't remember the exact words, nothing memorized this time, but I did ask God for healing.

When my tears dried, I felt differently. I couldn't explain the feeling-maybe confident? Bold but relaxed. I now believe the feeling was healing. It was how a person felt when she was healed. At the next appointment which would decide my fate, the doctor again brandished a protractor to measure the back x-ray. He checked the math twice then indicated that my curve had decreased, improved by seven degrees. The back brace stayed at bay.

I was later released from the doctor, brace-free. With therapeutic stretches, life changes, and intense workouts, I had earned the positive prognosis. But I felt that the moment I had lain prone on the floor and asked God to heal me, was the day my spine actually straightened. That, I did not earn.

Rescued from the back brace, I instead received braces on my teeth. I was still laser-focused on my health and kept up the exercise routine, if only for vanity reasons. I did not have time for shenanigans like the ice cream man's pestering calls. Once he called during my workout and that was the time I blew his cover. All it took was one mention of Michelle.

"I know who you are, ice cream man. Stop calling me!" I sounded braver than I felt when I slammed down the phone. But my outburst worked and I received a one year reprieve from the ice cream man. I was growing up and ready to stand my ground. When the going got tough, the tough got growing.

Bullburger Basics

*Note: Because the Bullburger was made fresh daily in a large wash tub, precise amounts and measurements aren't available.

Basic ingredients:
Beef and Sausage pressed through a grinder
3-4 eggs, whisked in a bowl
2-3 cups crumbled stale buns (filler)
Vinegar-based barbeque sauce
Salt and Pepper

Directions: Prepare hamburger patties by squishing above ingredients in aluminum bowl. Grill burgers in lots of melted butter. Keep a brush nearby to baste the burgers with even more butter. Cook until done. Top with grilled onions and place on largest hamburger buns you can find.

Papa on the far right. Dugout deliveries by scooters.

Me playing in the wine cellar

Grandmother and Papa Van Meter

Picture Day – Standing on trailer lot #6

Brother Michael and I with train tracks beyond the trees

OMU Will always be the Steel Mill to me

A photo bomb and sea horse ride at Santa Claus Land

Big O Barge!

Pop Warner Cardinals

Darrell Waltrip Fan Club

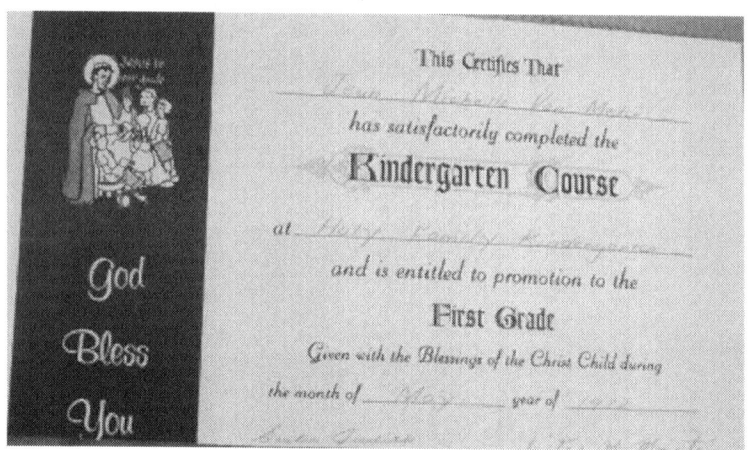

The afternoon class

My Grandmother's Childhood home on Griffith Ave.

Union Station today

Concrete Possum on a Concrete Tree

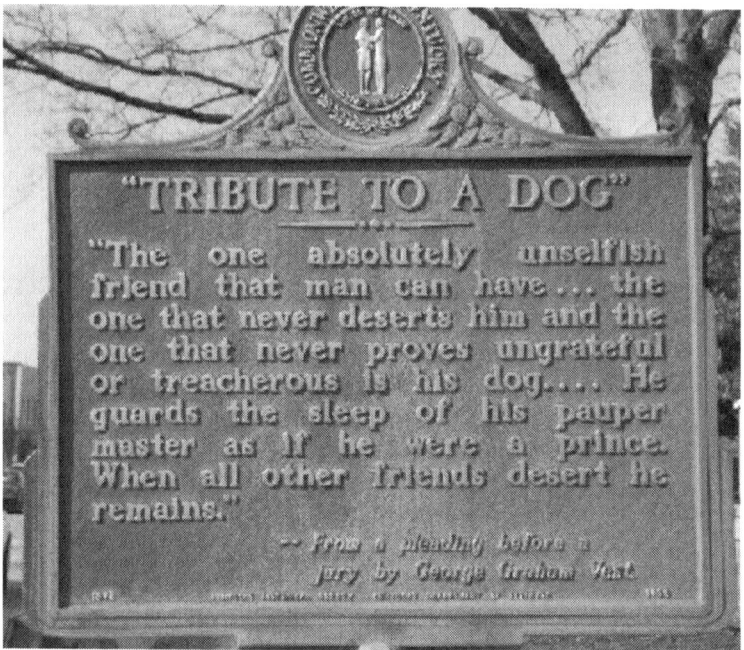

In front of our Courthouse

The Confederate Soldier Memorial

Catholic High

Gabe's Tower today

Memaw and Papaw Collignon

Papaw's Guitar

Mom, Dad, and me, 1966

My siblings and I at my wedding, 1989

MY BIG O JOURNEY

14

LET THE GAMES BEGIN

By seventh grade, birthdays transformed into boy-girl parties, hosted in a one-car garage or basement. Boys and girls had always attended parties together, but the designated name change indicated these particular parties had a precise purpose during puberty. A successful boy-girl party morphed into a make-out party by the end of the evening.

This was where the real courting began, except we called it going together. "So-n-so wants to know if you'll go with him." It made sense to answer, "To where?" If the question was in note form, you checked yes or no. The best of birthdays were ruined with a simple checkmark in the wrong box. Spin the bottle was the prime instigating game. Players sat in a circle while each took a turn spinning the bottle in the center. Whoever was at the pointed end of the bottle kissed the bottle spinner. This game was rigged, but if it didn't work as planned, Truth or Dare did the trick. You were dared to kiss someone, but the dare was arranged ahead of time by your best friend. With a dare, you found who your true friends were.

More physical games followed as we grew older. Kick ball on asphalt was a daily sport. Our uniform dress jumpers were not conducive to that game, or any game. We skidded into base with our slick shoes, even into other players, while flashing everyone for one lousy point. Choosing sides meant rejection for the same people over and over again. Players were chosen based on who had the biggest foot. For many, the shoe would never fit.

Lenny revisits picnic spot at the sewer ditch

Kick ball transformed into Kick the Can, played at nighttime by a neighborhood mob. With two mass teams, the team who was 'it' chased down every member of the other team in hiding. Those captured were placed in a jail near a tin can which sat in the middle of the street. When an uncaught team member kicked the can, all the prisoners were set free. My curfew ended before the game did.

The older we grew, the lazier the games. Four Square was more our speed. Instead of running pell-mell, we maintained a ball in a little square chalked onto the cement. Sweating was optional. These low-key games were the next step in preparing us for the video game craze ahead. They prepared the boys anyway. Girls had no interest in video games outside from the occasional Pong or if brother happened to misplace the handheld football game. My mind can still conjure up Pong's sound effects-sounded like a submarine.

Boys were quickly addicted to the video games. After every football game, both teams of boys headed to the Pizza Hut across from Union Station. While the cheerleaders enjoyed the juke box and pan pizza with pitchers of Dr. Pepper, the football players fought over the Ms. Pac-Man game next to the salad bar, neglecting both girls and grub.

Weekends were worse. All the Heavy-Duty bikes in Owensboro were parked at the entrance to Mr. Wiggs department store in Wesleyan Park Plaza. The bike riders never saw the inside of the store, but stayed in the foyer where the waiting line for the Space Invaders game commenced. Girls were too cool to ride bikes at this time, so parents dropped us off at Grants, the other anchor store, or nearby Sir Beef from which we could walk to Mr. Wiggs. Either was preferable to a direct drop-off; we hid parents from view as much as possible. These Saturdays were wasted watching boys play video games, and what fun it was. We were too old to ride bikes, but bored enough to spend all our quarters riding the horsey in front of Mr. Wiggs…anything to get the boys' attention.

This was the same time when perms became popular hairstyles. The bigger the hair, surely the boys would notice us. Hair was teased to extremes and bangs became wings. If fly-away bangs were not plastered down with Aqua Net hairspray, chances of becoming airborne were high.

Boys further lost interest in girls when the 42nd Street arcade opened. Girls enjoyed some of the games like Air Hockey and Foosball, but mainly we stayed on one floor while the boys stayed on another, lost in the buzzes and bleeps of video games. The one-hit wonder song, Video Killed the Radio Star was released to commiserate the plight of teenage girls around the world at this time.

15

A TEEN IN TOWNE SQUARE

I was raised with The Brady Bunch show and could recount every episode from the one where Tiger was lost to the one in Hawaii with the tarantula. "The story of a lovely lady who was bringing up three very lovely girls" was played by Florence Henderson from Owensboro. 'Mrs. Brady' sometimes gave kudos to her hometown while on the show. I would later graduate from Ms. Henderson's same high school alma mater.

My favorite episode was when Marcia busted her nose and "something suddenly came up" for poor Marcia, Marcia, Marcia. My next favorite was when Bobby and Cindy set out to break the world's record on the see-saw. This one show inspired me the most. We didn't have a see-saw, just a teeter-totter that came with the swing set. Teeter-totters were good for nothing except pinching fingers. We fought daily over the two swings, but never the teeter-totter. See-saws were hard to come by, found only in a few parks. It couldn't be because they made perfect catapults for little sisters. When hopping off one see-saw end, you see your sister fly up, and then you saw her land=see-saw.

I tried to find something I was good at, close to home. I was too big for my brother's Big Wheel and the 'Inchworm, Inchworm, I love you' had creaked its last as it sagged to the ground. I could skateboard on my banana-shaped board, which had a permanent outline of a black foot on it from riding barefooted. My other toy of choice was the pogo stick, that or the hula-hoop.

Then, we lived and breathed by The Guinness Book of World Records. It was better than Who's Who in America to have our name listed in the record breaker's Bible. The world record for pogo jumping was twenty hours and thirteen minutes.

I only fell short of the record by eight hours. When my dad left for work in his pea green Gran Torino, which resembled a smashed truck, I was hopping like the Energizer Bunny. When Dad came home for lunch, I was still hopping four hours later. I only asked for the basic food staple-a peanut butter and jelly sandwich to be brought to the curb. Dad never asked, "White or wheat?" White bread was the only way to go. Anything that wasn't pure white, like the crust or the first piece we called the hill, was tossed to the birds. Dad should have asked me, "Why are you eating peanut butter while on a pogo stick?" It was the perfect set-up for a Reese's commercial: "Hey, you got peanut butter in my chocolate."

"No, you got chocolate in my peanut butter." We could have made a fortune if we had pogoed with peanut butter first.

Hopping for hours was the closest I ever came to

breaking any record, except when I and one other person contracted Rocky Mountain spotted fever in a given year. When my pogo stick was put to rest, childish activities were passed over for more grown-up girl deeds. Like other teenagers in town, I liked to shop. It was a subtle change from hopping until I dropped to shopping until I dropped.

To shop, we ventured Downtown to Andersons and McAtee's department stores. Famous Name knit slacks were only $1.99, but they never told you that famous name because knit pants were a passing fad and designers did not want their name attached. Stirrup pants soon emerged. Waistline elastic held the pants up but the stirrups around the ankles pulled them down. We made it through these and other fads like the poncho and gaucho phase which made ladies look like miniature mariachis.

The Interstate store fulfilled our school uniform needs. Wearing a gingham jumper for eight years and then a plain brown skirt for another four was enough to be arrested by the fashion police. To spruce up school uniforms, we donned Adidas or Puma terry cloth jackets with them. Later, those jackets became silk ones. Mine was blue and it debuted at the Shaun Cassidy concert at Robert's Stadium in Evansville. I wore it when Shaun sang the sexy song, Da Doo Run Run. When silk jackets retired, the rabbit fur coat was Santa's favorite gift to give.

The jean scene was found at Dizzy Dave's in an airplane hangar building. Owensboro had two hospitals at the time, "County" and "Mercy." Dizzy Dave's was located across the road from the County one. Stockpiles of blue jeans from the ground to the rounded ceiling towered over the jungle of jeans on round racks. With countless jeans, the store was difficult to maneuver, and the curtained dressing rooms had long waiting lines. Jean sales rocketed when the baggies fad faded into the trendy straight-legged jeans. The new jeans were so straight that toes had to be pointed precisely to try them on. Stiff-legged teens walked robotically around the Dizzy Dave's store as if they had peed in their pants.

For upper body apparel, a teensy alligator on the lapel of sports shirts announced the preppy fad, 'prep' for short. Fancy topsider shoes or penny loafers with a real penny in the shoe tongue finished the look from head to toe. Not only did we have to learn to walk in stiff jeans, we had to keep our pennies in place. But we looked good while doing it.

I couldn't recall a pre-mall Owensboro. Lincoln Mall was always there with a water fountain filled with pennies that we pulled from our penny loafers. Woolco anchored the mall with the Mall Twin Cinema at the other end. The theater was often sold-out for movies like Jaws, The Deep, and Friday the 13th-part 20. There was no such thing as PG-13 movies, so we were often forced to sneak into the Rated R movies.

Movie ushers dressed to the nines with suits and bowties, but acted more like bouncers. They were in the same category as roller rink guards and librarians. If you put your feet on the chair in front, the ushers bounced you out the exit door. If you were discreet, they turned the other way when you snuck into a better movie and shared a seat with your best friend, as long as you patronized the concession stand for overpriced Jordan Almonds and Goo Goo Clusters. We were so thin that it took two of us skinny girls to hold down the movie seats anyway.

I was once bedazzled by a Sarah Coventry necklace at

the Lincoln Mall jewelry store. Stick pins were the rage then-sticks with pins on the back. I preferred the pins with a Christmas tree or anchor figure on top. Ten different pins could fit on a turtleneck sweater. When pins went out of style, a cubic zirconia ring became a girl's best friend. These pieces soon became vintage jewelry. Lincoln Mall became vintage too, when the new mall ventured into town.

Towne Square Mall opened in Owensboro during one of the worst snow storms Owensboro ever had. At the grand opening, cars backed up for miles on the busy Frederica Street, before the back entrance to the mall was constructed off of Carter Road. Bacon's was the premier department store, while Jean Nicole was the teenybopper's boutique of choice. Even Santa changed venues and moved his sled from the downtown Sears to Towne Square Mall's central clock. An escalator was the only missing motif. It was asking too much for architects to construct an escalator for a one story building.

Parents dropped off kids at the mall entrance and left

them there for the weekend until school restarted on Monday. That was the way it seemed anyway, but we didn't mind. Kidnapping was not a real threat in Owensboro since most families already had a tribe of children and were not interested in raising more.

Osco Drugs was next to Morrison's Cafeteria. From the drugstore, we purchased Lifesavers candy books for friends. For a best friend's Christmas gift, we found a birthstone necklace or a mood ring at Spencer's. Enough money was left for one giant Hershey's Kiss for some undeserving boy. I saturated the Christmas card attached to the chocolate kiss in red lipstick kisses and spelled "SWAK" on the envelope-that meant sealed with a kiss, as if he couldn't tell.

The rest of the envelope was covered in LOL which stood for "Lots of Love" back then. Imagine my apprehension years later when email entered the scene with men, women, and children alike ending every sentence with LOL. I felt uneasy toward the men, thinking their emails inappropriate, while still assuming that LOL stood for "Lots of Love." Evidently, the unsuspecting boy who received the special Christmas card from me thought so too and fled the scene between Christmas and Valentine's Day. I usually ate the Hershey's kiss alone on New Year's Eve. It was nothing to laugh out loud about.

SHELLY VAN METER MILLER

16

SLEEP IN PEACE

"Do you remember the Easter morning murder?

"It was so sad. Let's not talk about that."
"I thought it happened a long time ago"
"Yes, but it tore the town up."

By the time my recent phone conversation with Mom took place, the murdered victim had been dead for over forty years. I was just five years old when the 1972 Owensboro murder happened. However, the passing of time had no effect on the online forums regarding the victim's demise. They were still alive and well.

Poking around the dormant past awakened old tensions. Unanswered questions with unspeakable answers could still tear the town up. The actual scene of this murder mystery was bulldozed to make way for a student parking lot. That was one way to pave over the past. But the past had its way of extracting the truth, nothing but the truth, so help us, God. Mom was right. Let's not talk about this one.

The seventies crime scene with its dark alley and long hill did not represent the essence of Owensboro, although it did represent some of our sleepovers while growing up. Our youthful crime solving skills derived from Nancy Drew mystery books, combined with boldness from the banned Judy Blume books, led us to believe we could make a difference. Once, at midnight, a group of girls snuck upstairs from the sleepover basement on McCreary Avenue, to the basement stairs of nearby Longfellow School, where the hush-hush murder happened seven years before. I never took part, but not because I was Sandra Dee. I refused to go because boys were not involved. I was not interested in sneaking out with just girls because I was a chicken with a capital 'C' about ghosts with a capital 'G'. When all was over but the squealing, the escapees accomplished nothing but scaring themselves.

Sleepover hors d'oeuvres of stovetop Jiffy Popcorn, and TV dinners from tin trays were shared, along with chips and dip. Freedom meant plopping as much dip as I could on one chip. In my own family of six, that was not an option. Double dipping was not frowned upon amongst girlfriends though. Afterwards, we retreated to the basement for big girl stuff like prank phone calls, music, and more ghost stories. Drooling over Leif Garrett and Robby Benson in the Tiger Beat Magazine was standard procedure.

We wore ourselves out with contests while dancing "the bump" and crooning to the Bay City Rollers, K.C. and the Sunshine Band, and KISS. Music records cost a whole 99 cents at Wax Works. We toted entire record collections from house to house like travelling iPods. Records were often scratched because of this, but another cent did the trick when we taped a penny to the record player's needle. It then played over the scratched track and did not break our dance rhythm that we imitated from American Bandstand and Soul Train.

Adding to our sleepover delight, pop star Michael Jackson had dance moves which were totally Off the Wall. The Bump went out the door when the Moonwalk walked in. With our Kodak cameras, we captured the action with square disposable flashes which fried the faces on the photos, making the party scene indistinguishable.

When my neighbors, Carol and Angie had a sleepover, we camped in their dad's car in the driveway. He owned a CB radio which we tuned in regularly to learn colorful cuss words. We added "ten-four" sometimes from our collectively shared handle of 'Baby Blue.' While truckers kept on truckin', they were unaware that our convoy never left the driveway.

The same neighbors drove a van which was not a mini-van, but rather a van with mini-blinds. Its endless passenger capacity steered us everywhere from Taco John's to order Oles with extra seasoning, to Long John Silver's to order just the seasoning. For only a quarter, the crispies fried in fish grease could be just the grease, please. Anything was edible when smothered in ketchup. For one more quarter, we splurged on a soft-serve ice cream cone. Such delicacies were served with Coke. No matter if it was Pepsi or Dr. Pepper, it was still Coke. Tab was the only other soda distinction until we heard it gave cancer to rats. Then we were back to Coke.

During sleepovers, whoever fell asleep first was a

victim. Her hand was placed in cold water to make her wet her pants and her training bra was frozen in the freezer to make her cry. It wasn't a real slumber party until someone cried. When tears put a damper on things, we rehashed ghost stories to liven the mood.

I could tell a mean ghost story during sleepovers, made scarier by a bare lightbulb in the basement or total blackout except for a flashlight on my face. I was afraid of some of my own stories, like the haunting at Ben Hawes State Park. Forget Close-ups, I was hesitant to put my money where my mouth was when it came to actually living out the tale. Thankfully, no sane adult drove us to the park in the middle of the night to appease overactive imaginations.

When crossing railroad tracks, we generally held up our feet for good luck. On the tracks at Ben Hawes, we stopped in the middle and waited to be pushed off the tracks. Legend had it that a school bus of kids once stopped before the tracks and was hit by a train. According to the story, if a car parked on the tracks, the ghosts of kids would move it off the tracks. Sprinkling baby powder on the back bumper could capture the ghosts' handprints. When we made it off the tracks without getting hit by a real train, we always checked the bumper. Somehow we survived our own ghost stories and live to walk amongst everyone today.

We believed another story from Ben Hawes Park. During the eighteenth century, a woman was burned at the stake for witchcraft. If you waited quietly in the park's bushes, you could witness the night torches of those trekking up the hill to burn her. I put my faith in the legend instead of the 'seeing is believing' stance and was not a proponent of audience participation for this one.

I told the tales, but a ghost hunter I would never be. Looking back, it was not the dead people I should have feared, but the live ones. Over time, real crimes were committed in the area, crimes committed by live people who did not leave fingerprints in baby powder.

As the slumber party wound down to the crooning of a Barry Manilow album, we brought out the hair brushes. This ritual only worked in a sleepover setting and should not be tried at home. When Mom brushed my hair, she scored my part with a comb I swore was a knife, separating individual hairs to their proper side while tugging at the strays which wouldn't behave. Hairs which floated in static were dampened with cold water, giving me chills. Inevitably, a 'rat' was found underneath my blonde mane. I saw the relentless rats in the brush when Mom extracted them. By the next morning, they were back.

Hair brushing at sleepovers was different. The motion of brushing left girls in a catatonic trance. My scalp tingled as another brushed my hair. The brush bristles felt like a massage around my ears. The gentle tugs made me quiver not shiver. It actually felt good when head lice were transferred from person-to-person. The Mom Brigade dealt with the consequences of cooties the next morning when their phone chain pinned the blame of head lice on the sleepover. No one ever took the initial responsibility for a louse in the house.

In the meantime, I curled up in my Snoopy sleeping bag, wide awake from the spooky tales, caffeinated Cokes, and crawling cooties. It wasn't until the sun came up that I could finally sleep in peace. I wished all could rest in peace.

17

HARD GREEN TOMATOES

Friends called him Jack. My best friend called him Daddy. I called him Mr. Hicks, and the rest of the town called him Coach. While a growing teen, I was the Eddie Haskell of Owensboro who showed up promptly at six o' clock every Friday evening at Jack Hick's supper table. He thought it was for the steak dinner with A-1 sauce, but really it was for the sweet tea.

The Hicks' sweet tea had a secret ingredient that had nothing to do with taking the instant Nestea plunge. I thought surely the rest of Owensboro would catch on to the specialty drink by now, but when I dined out recently and asked for sweet tea, the waitress said, "Is it okay if I bring unsweet tea with sugar packets and you can sweeten it yourself?"

"Sure, if Monopoly money is okay with you," I answered.

Sweet tea was just one of the sweet memories in the Hick's home. I would walk several blocks to their house and enter through the single car garage. No friend ever used the front door. I first met Mrs. Hicks in the kitchen chair, reading a new book, and then Mr. Hicks in the next room, on the loveseat watching TV or Mr. Robinson mowing the yard behind him. The teapot whistled on the stove as I tromped up the stairs to find my best friend plotting our escape plan for the evening.

"Sneaking out" was what we called it and that's precisely what we did. At a certain hour every Friday evening, we pretended to be ladies in waiting. Watching from the upstairs window, we waited until the boys lined up below to catch us. Without cell phones, the timing had to be well-synched and planning ahead was a must.

The game plan went like this: Crack the window to test the antennae pole for sturdiness. Would it hold one girl at a time to shimmy down the pole? Check. Who would be there to catch the fall? Boys. Check. What would we do once we snuck out? Throw tomatoes at cars and tip over dumpster at Immaculate School. Hold up.

My dad was on the clean-up crew after last week's dumpster dump. I was a no-go. Could the boys possibly swing by to catch my window leap after they tipped the trash? And what was with the tomatoes? Usually we festooned yards in toilet paper. Or, we threw eggs or other breakfast fare at cars. Raw biscuits stuck to things easily, especially to stop lights. I once saw a biscuit bake before my eyes while stuck to a red light. It seemed a little early in the season for tomatoes though.

The ladies in waiting got tired of waiting sometimes. The 'boys will be boys' often got sidetracked and only came for the girls once their fun was over. We thought this was another one of those nights we would be marooned in the upstairs bedroom until we heard a knock at the Hick's front door. Immediately, we knew it wasn't one of us. The two policemen on the doorstep may have been the first people to ever knock at that door. But the cops did know Mr. Hicks, probably when he was their baseball coach.

As they all shook hands, we ladies waited quietly, halfway down the stairs so we could hear every word. From the police report, a lady's windshield was broken as she was driving on the next street. A green tomato lay in her lap. We were startled when Mr. Hicks yelled up the stairs because we were already well within ear shot.

One policeman asked us, "Do you ladies know anything about kids throwing tomatoes at cars on Citation?"

Stacy and I looked at each other feigning surprise. We acted as if we spent every Friday night locked away upstairs. How could two innocent girls know anything about juvenile delinquents in the neighborhood? And also, we've never seen those boys under the window trying to get us to jump either.

I spoke first. "No, sorry we can't help."

After an awkward silence, Mr. Hicks glanced at me and spoke to the two men. "If she says she doesn't know, then she is speaking the truth."

Stacy and I were released to go upstairs, back to our situation room. We stewed around awhile trying to justify the lie and waited unsuccessfully for the lie to become the truth like it sometimes did. Once the door shut behind the policemen, instead of instant relief, we felt remorse. Then I said what we both dreaded, "I can't lie to your dad."

I had no qualms about lying to the police, although I had been raised better than that. It was a tug-of-war between the two virtues of honesty and loyalty which confounded me. I found myself mad at the boys for potentially ruining the night and not having enough sense to use ripe tomatoes. And for the first time ever, I found that my word was tied to someone else's honor. Mr. Hicks was a well-respected man in the community and I couldn't disrespect him with my lies. He not only believed me, but he believed in me. And there lie the difference, although this pun was no fun.

After we confessed to Mr. Hicks, he bore our shame and recalled the policemen, this time with the truth. We did not have to stand and face the law. Mr. Hicks handled the truth by handling the officers for us. We never heard about it again. I bet he was pleased that honesty prevailed, and also pleased to get the names of the boys who threw the tomatoes. Mr. Hicks was always scouting for good pitchers for his American Legion baseball team.

Stacy and I had mixed emotions. We felt bad for ratting out our friends, but good for telling the truth to authorities. Heaven forbid we wear goody-two-shoes for too long though. The label lingered only a moment on our willing feet which were ready to jump into action.

"Should we still try to sneak out tonight?" Stacy asked.

"We could. It's not like the cops are going to come here for a third time tonight," I said. Besides, they would be too busy playing good cop/bad cop with our boyfriends.

We pondered the idea before our final answer. Nah,

there would be no boys now, so what was the point? There would be plenty of other nights. Eventually, we wore out the antennae pole at the Hick's house. Mr. Hicks probably tired of adjusting the TV rabbit ears while watching sports. Meanwhile, we were usually safe on the ground.

The more we snuck out, the braver we became-even when out of town. No matter what town we were in, we could always find boys willing to catch us from an upper story window. Once, my girlfriends and I visited my aunt in Louisville. It was always a treat for us to eat at Chi chi's Mexican restaurant and then see a concert in the big city.

Peter Frampton was live at the arena. Aunt Charlotte dropped us at the stadium for the concert, so we were in the mosh pit by ourselves. We borrowed cigarette lighters from whoever's parents smoked so we could wave them in the air in the hopes of making the concert begin sooner than scheduled. We believed that if the song artist saw the lights and heard the screaming, he would sing more songs. I was lost in the squealing crowd, counting on Peter to "Show Me the Way." In the mosh pit, I was focused on keeping my long hair from catching on fire from the swaying lighters when a stranger threw up his hotdog on my tennis shoe. The hotdog encounter put a glitch in our sneak-out plan for the evening. I would not sneak out while wearing a hotdog on my shoe.

The first thing we noticed when visiting Aunt Charlotte was the cute boys who lived in the same apartment complex. The whole scenario appeared to be easier than we were used to, closer proximity anyway. We even enlisted another conspirator into our ranks.

Our friend, Lisa was sucked into our sneak out regime. As usual, the time and place for sneaking out was arranged in advance, with the boys only having to show up. All went according to plan until Aunt Charlotte showed up alongside the boys at the secret rendezvous.

In the morning, Aunt Charlotte sent Stacy, Lisa, and me packing. She introduced us to the Greyhound bus station and even bought our tickets. At 10:00 A.M. I found myself on a public bus for the first time, along with my comrades. We shared one bench while senior citizens took up all the other seats. The bus took the scenic route and stopped at every Mom and Pop restaurant between Louisville and Owensboro. Between us girls, we pooled our cash to share French fries for lunch. It was our only food staple for five hours.

Like the boys who threw the tomatoes, I knew what it felt like to be thrown under the bus, only I was thrown on it. The extended bus trip got me thinking though. That, and the next time we snuck out when Nancy smashed her glasses.

We were extra sneaky when sneaking out with a car. From The Sound of Music movie, we got the idea to shift the gears into neutral while pushing the car out of hearing distance from the house. It worked fine until Nancy's glasses fell in the street during the pushing. We heard a crunch as the back tires squashed her prescription glasses. This wasn't just Nancy's problem; Nancy was the only licensed driver in our group.

We assured her we would "help" her drive. We grabbed the steering wheel and sometimes warned, "Stop at this one. It's red." Sneaking out was becoming too much trouble. We were too coy to be getting caught so often. The best of plans were jeopardized when a mother searched for a hairdryer and called another mother to speak with her own daughter as to the hairdryer's whereabouts. When she heard, "She's not here. I thought they were all staying at so-n-so's house," this triggered the mom phone chain: "I thought she was with you," and so forth. In the end, our evening plans were foiled, as were many more evenings which followed our groundings.

I was convinced my parents were in cahoots with a higher authority and prayed that special parent prayer, the one that never failed: "Lord, let her get caught for everything bad thing she does." This prayer worked wonders and I would use it on my own children someday. In the meantime, my friends and I decided to hang up our bad habit of sneaking out until the following year. We would be in junior high then.

18

DRIVE-INS AND DINERS

When I wasn't at the Boogie Shack teen hangout, dancing to Kool and the Gang's Celebration, and partying like it was 1999, I was at the movies. My peer group was a generation of movie-goers and especially enjoyed the drive-ins. We could hardly see the movies from the inside of a car trunk though. Sometimes we lay low until intermission before the coast was clear to exit the vehicle. Trunk loads of ticket dodgers filled the interiors of most Monte Carlo and Cutlass Supreme car trunks at the drive-in movies. Once the ticket booth attendants wised up to our trunk-or-treat schemes, we had to find an alternate route to sneak into the Star-lite Drive-in.

Via Shively Park, we trudged through the corn field which separated the park from the theater. After mapping out the corn maze, we found our way to a concrete block with a movie speaker on it, and tuned in to hear the otherwise silent movie on the screen. Paid customers offered their cars for comfort, but most of us preferred to huddle around the concrete blocks while drinking lukewarm Stroh's beer or Southern Comfort from a brown paper sack. This was our version of a block party, except the girls were more refined and drank Peppermint Schnapps on the rocks. Not many things tasted the same going down as they did when thrown up. That was classy.

Again, the ticket takers were on to our creative tactics to avoid paying for their parking lot. Additional drive-in employees were hired to work the corn fields which surrounded the drive-in theater. Their new job descriptions were to guard the fields by night and hunt down any movie seekers trying to make a run for it through the corn. It always came down to the corn.

There was nothing more frightening than getting chased through a corn field by a disgruntled employee trying to nab your money. Groups were separated during the chase so you never knew if the heavy breathing behind you was a friend or foe.

I tried to keep my eyes on the prize, the big screen in front of me. But the corn was never ending. Just when I got past a corn stalk slapping me in the face, another one popped up in its place. I was in a human whack-a-mole game with a whacker hot on my heels. I ran like a flapping bird trying to escape and even crawled like a mole to get out.

After we safely made it out of the corn, we made out in the corn. A boy waited just long enough for a girl to catch her breath before luring her back into the maze to make out. Cornfields, Little Hurricane's boat ramp, and Haunted Hill were the only options for parking and making out. Here was a convenient cornfield right next to the drive-in, with no additional driving. Kissing in a cornfield was still considered parking, even if the car was parked somewhere else. At the Star-lite, it was impossible to tell who was running into the corn and who was running out.

When my own teenage girls begged to go a cornfield maze during Halloween, I had to wonder at the hefty entrance fee. They paid good money to run through the maze while being chased by a masked person. I said, "You paid how much for a stranger to chase you through the corn?"

I thought back to the exhausted drive-in employees. Perhaps they found a more financially rewarding venture of chasing kids through corn mazes now. Drive-in theaters were making a comeback too. A movie combo with popcorn and a high speed cornfield chase might be the key to success.

When the Star-lite lost its twinkle, nearby Moonlite still shined. Directions to the still booming Moonlite proved unnecessary in the sunlight or moonlight. Upon entering the city of Owensboro, a visitor followed his nose to the rich smell of hickory wood, tinged with the tangy aroma of Worcestershire sauce, seasoned with brown sugar and vinegar. His nose steered the rest of his body into the infinite blacktop parking lot of Moonlite, short for the local eatery's proper name of the Moonlite Bar-B-Que Inn.

Before being seated inside the restaurant, a waitress asked, "Ya'll going' buffet?" The correct answer was "Yes." Moonlite did not need menus. I was certain you couldn't find both sliced and pulled mutton, ribs, country ham, burgoo, barbeque chicken, and banana pudding on any other daily buffet in America.

At Moonlite, mutton was still king. Our ancestors cooked the meat from a fat ewe and called it mutton. A century later, Moonlite Bar-B-Que was one of the few carrying on the tradition of the ewe. Originally a roadside stand, Moonlite now served 10,000 pounds of sheep per week-ten percent of all fat ewes in our nation. The mutton was served on a bun with pickle and onion. Special sauce could be added by the customer. Moonlite sold, on average, fifty of these sandwiches every day. On seasonal specials, one person ordered 150 sandwiches alone. I call that a glutton for mutton.

Burgoo was another Moonlite specialty, served at our church picnics and family get-togethers. We even served burgoo for Thanksgiving. The stew was not as complicated as it sounded: Vegetable soup + Mutton stew = Burgoo. The contents went into the pot in a certain order, while cooks stirred it all day in big vats, before selling the burgoo by the gallons. You knew it was good when your spoon stood up in it.

Moonlite lit up Owensboro and put it on the map, along with other barbecue joints like Old Hickory and the old Shady Rest. As if the barbeque capital of the world wasn't enough to house on Parrish Avenue, another establishment took the cue from Moonlite and let its little light shine like the Big Dipper in the sky. Indeed the next door's burgers at the Big Dipper drive-thru restaurant were out of this world. Folks at NASA agreed.

While recently visiting the Big O, I enjoyed a Dipper burger 'through the garden,' with some gems and a banana shake. 'Through the garden' was like rolling a hamburger through a garden, and picking up everything in its path to go on it. Gems were a fancy name for divine, crispy tater tots. I inhaled my meal for less than five dollars, while in a cramped parking lot in Kentucky. Meanwhile, a crew of space engineers impatiently awaited my arrival in Alabama. As they discussed experiment operations on the International Space Station, their main concern was long it would take for their Big Dipper hamburgers to land in Huntsville, Alabama. Based on their calculations, lunch would arrive in three hours and forty minutes, as soon as I finished eating mine and left Owensboro.

I sent a text message with a picture to my husband as he conferred with the rocket scientists. They heard the incoming text and turned to him as if to say, "Do we have lift-off?" Randy showed them the picture I took of Big Dipper's owner while out shopping in Owensboro. Their excitement peeked. The next picture I sent was of my own half-eaten burger. Now I was just being mean.

I had special written orders from the Alabama engineers. My purpose was to bootleg Big Dipper burgers across state lines, without sacrificing the quality of these burgers. All burgers were to be purchased plain, bun separated from burger, each burger individually wrapped in foil, all inside of a cooler. Special pickles were also stored in a separate container.

This precise process was meant to maintain the originality of the burger. Taste was at stake. The payment method may have involved money laundering too. The Big Dipper only accepted cash or Confederate gold, so the mathematical operation was considered well in advance by the same scientists. After careful calculations and horrendous Nashville traffic, the burgers made it safely to the NASA contractor in the allotted timeframe. As I smuggled the cooler past the guard, I could have sworn he radioed, "The Eagle has landed."

For sixty years, the Big Dipper made its mark in the lives of Owensboro citizens. A perpetual traffic jam existed on the West side of town, making Nashville's traffic a piece of cake. Parrish Avenue stayed backed up from hopeless drivers wishing to turn left into the Dipper's drive-thru. If I made a U-turn on Parrish and drove out of the way via the bypass, I could still turn right into the Big Dipper and beat those lefties every time. On my way there, I counted the cows in the closest pasture to see if the number decreased after I ordered my meal-that was how fresh the beef was.

In Grandmother's day, teenagers 'dragged' the Dipper. It wasn't really her time, but more like her son's time. Driving around in circles used to be called draggin,' then cruising,' and by my time, was called loitering. Grandmother only thought she was going for a burger on a Saturday night, but her son who was in the car, saw his buddies and begged my grandmother to get down on the floorboard. She did. She lay there long enough for him to drag the drive-thru three times before she craved a burger the next go-around. Apparently, cruising the Dipper alone was embarrassing enough, but preferable to cruising with your mother, who was bent like a pretzel. The things we would do for a good burger.

Grandmother liked her burgers, but preferred Gabe's for steak. Gabe's on Triplett Street was known as the "Steakhouse of the South." Open 24/7 and serving 1400 meals a day, it was no wonder. The elegant restaurant featured well-dressed waiters in what resembled tuxedo suits, serving well-dressed customers in pearls and patent leather shoes. The finest linen, china, and crystal made every candlelit meal a masterpiece. For this reason, Gabe's was a popular place for celebrations. Gabe's hosted Mom and Dad's wedding reception fifty years ago. Although they were just married and had exchanged wedding vows, Mom and Dad still went into separate rooms to change into their 'going away' outfits before leaving the reception.

At that time, no one left Owensboro without getting a glimpse of Gabe's Tower, which opened in 1963. The hotel was owned by the same Gabe of restaurant fame, and was shaped like a twelve story silo with a rooftop pool. A night at the tower was a one-of-a-kind vacation. There was no other hotel like it in the area, nor would there ever be again. Mom and Dad had their hearts set on Nashville and did not spend their wedding night at the tower. Instead of a valid driver's license to rent a hotel room, most hotels required a certified marriage license for a room reservation. Few hotels were as lenient as the 'no tell' motel across the bridge.

Papa liked the steak at Briarpatch, which was Kentucky Rib Eye at the time. We just called it 'Ribeyes,' naming the restaurant by the cut of beef it served. I rarely dined at steak restaurants until I was older. Rich cuisine was not wasted on children's cheap palettes. We did venture to eat out at places like Jerry's or Sambo's, across the street from each other on Frederica. But not on Fridays; Fridays meant fish. Roman Catholic parishes dotted most Owensboro neighborhoods, and fishy Fridays were a Lenten tradition.

For fried catfish, Red's was the place to be, an obscure cabin in Sorgho. I dreaded when I saw the hushpuppy basket go past because that meant the food was ready. I would rather play on the pinball machine in the front of the fish joint. Eating meant giving up my spot as the pinball wizard while kids waited in line to beat me or confiscate the extra pinballs in the shoot. Thank goodness for doggie bags or to-go boxes, invented for selfish children who wanted to play and then eat later. However, I did not eat the doggie bag fish the next day, on Saturday. Fish was for Friday and I didn't mess with tradition.

19

HOME OF THE BRAVE

Mark Twain once said, "It's not the size of the dog in the fight, it's the size of the fight in the dog." He might have been talking about Life on the Mississippi, but he also described life on the Ohio. There must be something in river water.

A historical marker stands at a straight shot from the river to the 2100 block of Frederica Street. The marker tells the tale of Grace Rash and her sassafras tree. On the right side of Owensboro's busiest street, drivers notice the marker before they notice the world's largest sassafras tree in the middle of the street, thanks to Grace's rashness in saving the tree from certain doom. When construction workers threatened to bulldoze the tree during a 1957 expansion of Frederica Street, Grace leaned against her prized sassafras with shotgun in hand. I pictured her aiming it at a worker a time or two before the governor of Kentucky was reached to 'pardon' the tree.

Because of the size of her fight, the sassafras survived and Frederica Street was built around it. The national champion tree still stands nearly one hundred feet tall with a wide berth of over twenty-two feet in circumference. Despite surviving the root beer craze, the sassafras' roots would not have survived paving for progress if it had not been for Ms. Rash speaking softly and carrying a big stick, one with bullets in it.

I remembered my Owensboro roots when my neighbor's tree cutters went on a killing spree of chopping down native pines. One tree straddled our property lines, a mature and majestic pine too wide for the tree hugger in me to hug. I looked out the window to see two chainsaws barking up the wrong tree, my tree. I stormed into the yard and wagged my own big stick, which was really my pointer finger. "Drop 'em now!" I threatened.

"We're just cutting off some dead limbs trying to help this tree out," the tree cutters said. They stopped talking when they saw that I was prepared to fight like a girl. I thought of Grace Rash. "Let me help you off my property," I said a little rashly. On a side note, the infamous Hatfield-McCoy feud began in my home state. Its origin was unknown, but it was possible a tree was involved.

My pine tree lived without involving the governor of Alabama. As a heavy-weight champion of the world once said, "There are no pleasures in a fight but some of my fights have been a pleasure to win"-Muhammad Ali (who is also from Kentucky).

One of the last battles of the Revolutionary War was fought in Kentucky as well. That was not surprising, but the fact that the Battle of Blue Lick occurred ten months after Lord Cornwallis surrendered at Yorktown was. There, brave men responded to a cry of, "Them that ain't cowards, follow me." Even famous frontiersman, Daniel Boone rose to the battle call at Blue Lick, knowing of the peril.

Boone said, "We are all slaughtered men," but crossed the river anyway. His own son died in that battle, and Daniel Boone was himself later buried in Frankfort, Kentucky. Some believed the picture on the Kentucky state flag was that of Daniel Boone shaking hands with a statesman. The men on our flag were flanked with the words "United We Stand, Divided We Fall."

The symbolic words were hailed from another war in which our state was indeed divided, the uncivil Civil War. Kentucky was the birthplace of both opposing presidents, Abraham Lincoln and Jefferson Davis. The Union's President Lincoln was born less than one hundred miles from Confederate President Davis. Both men were born a year apart, and both remembered their Kentucky heritage. Davis named his favorite horse

'Kentuck' and Lincoln's favorite song, Dixie, ironically became the anthem of the South. However, neither side showed favoritism to their old Kentucky home once the war started.

At this time in 1861, Owensboro was the home of a prominent lawyer, George Helm Yeaman. Yeaman soon moved up the ladder as a Daviess County judge and set his sights on the United States Congress. When Lincoln tried to pass the 13th amendment to abolish slavery, Yeaman was a congressman who opposed it. In a heated speech, Yeaman argued that if slaves were freed, they might someday vote, and women might get the idea that they could vote too. Congress booed this idea.

After Yeaman's presentation, President Lincoln called him into his office. Both men reminisced about Kentucky before Lincoln revealed the reason his father moved the family away. "A poor dirt farmer couldn't compete with slave plantations." Lincoln's boyhood home was just over the bridge on the Indiana side, close to my favorite Santa Claus Land, later renamed Holiday World.

Yeaman agreed with the farm issue but said he didn't think the nation was ready for emancipation. Lincoln said the nation was not ready for peace either, but would cross that bridge when it came. Lincoln's last plea: "I hope to have God on my side, but I must have Kentucky."

When the vote came to end slavery, Yeaman mumbled when it was his turn. He possibly said, "Yea, Man," under his breath. Then louder, he exclaimed, "Aye!" to the surprise of all. Owensboro's former judge cast the swing vote to abolish slavery. (Kentucky.com/2012/11/25)

And so the war began. Owensboro, itself, experienced

divisiveness and suffered the consequences during an 1865 raid, when soldiers had a layover in Owensboro. A bank robbery was foiled, but not without the capturing of thirteen Union prisoners whose bodies were burned before Rebels retreated to Tennessee.

As a paradox, one of Kentucky's first Confederate companies was raised at Owensboro, and three residents received Confederate Medals of Honor. A bronzed monument stands in Owensboro to honor these men. The man on the statue wears a slouch hat, but the slouch ends there. He depicts a Confederate soldier, ready for action with rifle in hand, standing guard over the Daviess County Courthouse lawn. Strangely, it was a band of Confederate raiders who torched the original courthouse due to wartime sentiments toward the African American Union soldiers stationed in Owensboro.

Fire was the Devil's friend and death was not so picky. The captain of the group of pyrotechnic marauders died of wounds he sustained while burning the courthouse. There, he fell and was buried on Kentucky soil. Sherman was right; war was Hell.

Around that time, a slave named Josiah Henson resided in Daviess County. Henson was the inspiration for Tom of Harriett Beecher Stowe's classic, Uncle Tom's Cabin. President Lincoln once said to Ms. Stowe, "Is this the little woman who made the Great War?" Stowe's fiction novel provoked wartime sentiments to an all-time high while based on the real life of a Maryland/Kentucky slave traded from farm-to-farm. My family claims a unique tie to Ms. Stowe's muse, Josiah Henson. Although difficult to prove and even harder to lift, our hewn wooden shelf used as a fireplace mantle, came from the property of Henson's slave quarters in Daviess County. The slave mantle then came with our property when we bought our suburban house, but we're not sure how it got there. I believe the story to be true because who would make up such a tale?

Owensboro did not miss a war. In 1923, one of Owensboro's most popular mayors was elected six times to the office, and encouraged the city council to rename an Owensboro park. Hickman Park was already named after him, James Hardin Hickman, but he opted to change the park's name to Legion Park in honor of Owensboro's American Legion who fought in World War I.

I grew up in the shade of Legion Park, playing on the witch's hat and tunneling down the tornado slide. The park was always in its present location, but was considered to be on the outskirts of town when it was designed. The park was accessible from the street car which ran every twenty minutes. Perhaps more memorable than a witch's hat and tornado slide, the park once boasted of a fishing pond, concession stand, and even a monkey house with two monkeys. The monkeys were gone before I came along. I definitely would have remembered them.

Kentucky residents were also among the Greatest Generation who fought in World War II. In true Kentucky spirit, Owensboro's scrap yard on Ninth Street filed for employee exemption from the draft, maintaining the business served the war effort. Employees were granted the exemption, but the company owner volunteered to serve his country overseas until 1945.

In that same Kentucky spirit, German POWs housed at Camp Breckinridge were forced to work in the tobacco fields, in place of Owensboro family members serving overseas. The POWs were responsible for building Union Station. In the typical German spirit, Union Station's outer walls were constructed to be sixteen inches thick, which explained how the station still stands today. The German prisoners of war were not mistreated in Kentucky. In fact, they were allowed to eat at several restaurants while their black American guards were not.

After Union Station was remodeled into a real estate business, my mother worked there while I was in high school. It was hard to imagine what a bustling town Owensboro had been up until 1958 with eighteen daily passenger trains coming and going from the station. Harry Truman even spoke at Union Station for his Whistle stop tour.

After World War II, a building boom took place in Owensboro. Some would argue the greatest contribution from the architectural firm of Johnson, Depp and Quisenberry was the building of our airport. Others suggested the great contribution from the same family was that of Owensboro's most famous actor, Johnny Depp, who lived on Stockton Drive until the age of three.

Another local family gave their great contribution during the Vietnam War. American hero, Col. Charles Shelton of Owensboro was shot down on his birthday during a reconnaissance mission over Laos. He safely parachuted and radioed his position, but weather prevented his rescue. By the time his records were made public he had been captured and held in a cave for three years. During that time, he never betrayed his country. He even killed some of his captors while handcuffed. This was unbeknownst to his family back in Owensboro, who was only told of his missing in action and later updated status to Prisoner of War.

Despite several rescue attempts, official records ended in a Hanoi prison when the Laotian government informed the family that Shelton was eaten by a tiger. Twenty-nine years after his capture, the paper trail ended. Days after what would have been their thirty-eighth wedding anniversary, Shelton's wife took her own life. She was buried in Arlington Cemetery, next to her husband's empty casket. Owensboro and America's hero was never put to rest. (Rick Allen, 11/11/2010)

Looking back through Owensboro's past, patriotic people had walked where I walked, maybe even sat on the same park benches. Heroes were in my midst, yet I rarely paused to read the dedications detailing my fellow citizens' heroic deeds. I appreciated those sacrifices, along with the ones I knew nothing about.

I made it a point to read the historical markers in Downtown Owensboro. Before trekking back to my parked car at the renovated Walgreen's building belonging to my dad's friend, I came upon my last sign in Smother's Park. It began: "The one absolutely unselfish friend that man can have..." The same marker ended: "When all other friends desert he remains." The sign was unique among those commemorating local heroes because the marker was entitled 'Tribute to a Dog.' Twain was right; it was about a dog fight.

I glanced upwards to a rooftop garden and walked the rest of the way with my head held high. Owensboro was the home of the brave. Both heroes and dogs had walked among us, and still did. Although it was Sitting Bull who said, "I wish it to be remembered that I was the last man of my tribe to surrender my rifle," this could have been said by any number of people from Owensboro-from Grace Rash to Col. Charles Shelton. Seeing how we fought to protect the rights of a tree, and those in foreign lands, you bet your sassafras we'd dare defend our own rights.

20

NO PARKING

By junior high, I had come a long way from the warped ideas I had regarding relationships, like those I formed during religion class. When the priest explained that kissing a boy was a sin because it led to other things, I was confused even after some brave soul asked the priest, "What if it doesn't lead to other things, then is kissing still a sin?"

The priest affirmed that kissing for an extended time could still be a sin. The explanation prompted another question, but I did not wish to raise my hand in class for the priest to elaborate. What did he mean by "extended?" The exact meaning was never established in my mind, so I applied my own made-up rules for making out or sinful kissing.

My safe kissing rule consisted of a time limit of ten consecutive seconds. So after the church ice cream social, I went behind the baseball dugout and kissed whomever I pleased for one, one-thousand, two, one-thousand, three, one-thousand four…all the way to ten seconds. After I counted to ten, I started a conversation until the boy shut me up by kissing me again. The good thing was that the count started over and the supplementary conversation bought me another ten seconds of kisses.

There soon came a time when I did not wish to talk between kisses and went to Confession regularly to wipe the slate clean. My parents had to wonder when I jumped on my bike every Saturday and said I was going to Confession. They should have followed behind me in the car. Thankfully, the church did away with the old Confessionals and used them as broom closets. It was possible they got tired of frightened kids using them for bathrooms. In the new Confession room, the priest was already waiting on the other side of the screen. Face-to-face Confession was an option, but not an option for me when I kissed overtime. As usual, I knelt down and emptied my guilty conscience of 'little' sins to warm-up before I dropped the bomb. I tried to slip the big sin in the middle, but placement did not matter.

"I broke one of the Commandments, um…the adultery one." I hurried on with more sins and continued nonchalantly, "I sassed my mom and didn't dust my room…for these and all my sins I am sorry," Silence. "I said I'm sorry," I whispered. More silence. My heart thumps matched my goose bumps. After my third "Sorry," the priest asked me to come out from behind the screen.

I almost pleaded, "Pay no attention to the girl behind the screen," except I wasn't Dorothy nor was he the Wizard. I could have passed for the Cowardly Lion though, when the priest and I sat face-to-face after all. He pulled the entire story out of me and then taught me the whole story of adultery. It was like getting slapped in the face by the upperclassman all over again. Our two versions did not match. "Oh no-I did not do that. No, definitely not that!"

Kissing school boys was a far cry from adultery. One would think after attending Mass six days per week I would know this. Instead I played, "Here's the church, here's the steeple, open the door, and here's all the people," with my clasped hands which were supposed to be praying. I did revive when I saw priest robes coming down the aisle to sprinkle holy water on sleepers. Maybe it was time I woke up and did not revolve my life around boys. I took a sabbatical from kissing.

THOU SHALT NOT PARK HERE

I became an Avon lady with a sales territory. Every two weeks, I toted a gigantic shoulder bag of samples while wearing blue eye-shadow, which only stopped because my eyebrows were in the way. I rang doorbells and said, "Ding-dong, Avon calling." Everyone received either Sweet Honesty perfume or Skin-so-Soft bath oil from me during gift-giving seasons. Most of my business was from the teachers at school.

I took up cheerleading again and made the junior varsity team. For fundraising, the cheerleaders sold cupcakes from individual shoeboxes that we carried from class to class. After daily plundering my own shoebox while averaging two Twinkies a day, along with Jungle Juice from the snack machine, I still had enough lunch money to split a salad with two friends, and spare change for Grippos chips after school. At cheer practice, I worked off the junk food by rolling my eyes at the coach. Sets of fifteen jumps were issued for punishment, and I received at least three sets a day for eye rolling. The eyes spoke a universal language.

One of the perks of cheerleading was the cheer room. Besides private lockers, we had access to the third story room during lunch. On nice days, we slipped out the cheer room window onto the roof of the adjacent building. Like cheerleaders on a hot tin roof, we rolled up our uniform skirts to get an amplified suntan reflected from the shingles. Our rooftop tanning beds were directly atop the principal's office, so we had to 'lay low' and gossip quietly. We did not consider the nun's convent across the courtyard, however. Once, the nuns spied us on the roof with our dresses rolled up. Our sunburned thighs were a dead giveaway. No more rooftop rendezvous.

It took a village of nuns and priests to keep us in line. Even neighbors took turns offering their parenting skills. Once, our neighbor, Mrs. Norcia, grounded me because she heard I snuck out yet again. I was grounded for two weeks from going to the Boogie Shack or she would tell my parents what I did. If Mom found out, she would threaten me with the Mount again.

The Mount, short for Mount St. Joseph Academy, was a boarding school for girls. I pictured it a Purgatory for bad girls by the way Mom used it against me. I faced my neighbor's grounding from a distance because I couldn't afford my parents finding out. It was challenging to convince them I preferred to spend two weekends in a row dusting my room, but if it meant the Mount, I would Pledge more often.

I avoided the Mount until I was pledged to be married. By then, the Mount's boarding school dissolved and its halls were used for retreats. After the grounds were renovated, I boarded at the Mount for an Engaged Encounter with my fiancé, both of us with private cells. It was a magical place with spacious grounds, and not the prison I imagined. But I'm getting ahead of myself.

21

THROWED UP

"Old age is like a plane flying through a storm. Once you're aboard, there's nothing you can do."-Golda Meir

Golda was right; that was exactly how I felt. But instead of a storm, Kentucky was in the middle of a drought. The surrounding states of Indiana and Missouri were as well, so I saw.

Although the land was parched, the air was soggy with humidity in late June. At the old Owensboro airport, you could drive your car right up to an airplane for curbside service. There was one building, one terminal, and probably just one airplane too. My relatives lived across the street from the airport. If I had wanted, I could have parked at their house and walked across the street to board an airplane. At least a chain link fence separated the airport from the residential area.

I had no business flying that day. I went to the airport to visit a high school buddy at his workplace. I found him in the reflective hangar shaped like a rainbow. He had forgotten about our appointment and had already made lunch plans at a restaurant I'd never heard of. He invited me to join him and his buddy.

"Who's driving?" I asked.

"Nobody. We're flying. Do you mind moving your car off the runway?"

My friend needed flight hours to earn his pilot's license and his lunch buddy was actually his flight instructor. I was just going along for the ride. Famous last words. Without giving it much thought, I crawled into the cubbyhole in the back of the plane and shoved the seatbelt out of the way. Airplane seat belts didn't make sense to me. A little strap could hardly compete with altitude or my attitude. I supposed that was why I entrusted my life to someone without a driver's license for the airplane too.

The drone of the plane's engines drowned out any second thoughts. I began to feel like the character, Tattoo, from Fantasy Island, but it did me little good to say, "The plane, the plane- I want out." Instead, I watched my world whisk past as we were cleared for take-off.

The plane ride was actually pleasant and relaxing. Blue skies stretched over a patchwork quilt of dehydrated farmlands below. The guys in the front seat forgot about me, which was fine. I did not want to interfere with flight lessons because if the pilot flunked the flight, it affected my wellbeing too. An airplane backseat driver I was not.

Both pilot and co-pilot pointed down to the cracked

ground which was once a body of water before the drought. Barges leaned lopsided along the shore, waiting for more water. I thought the flight instructor mouthed the word, "Mississippi," but that couldn't be right because the Mississippi River was somewhere near Mississippi, and we were supposed to be in Kentucky. I never could read lips though.

After hovering over the used-to-be river, we flew past some ragged corn fields. It was then that both pilot and co-pilot turned to me with raised eyebrows. They had just asked me a question, but unable to read lips, I didn't know how to answer. I gestured quickly anyway because I felt one of them should keep his eyes on the road, or clouds. I nodded 'yes' and smiled. Their eyebrows rose in surprise. So I gave them the thumbs-up sign to let them know I was having a good time. I hopefully showed enough enthusiasm so they would focus on steering the plane. The instructor nudged for me to locate my seatbelt as he made the motion of clicking it together. Oh-oh.

When I tightened my lap belt, the plane exploded through the air. I looked at my lap, surprised it was still there. I peered out my peephole window and panicked when I saw smoke. Then it cleared and turned blue. That would be the sky. My windpipe would not manage a breath and I had to swallow my scream. I felt my heart rise up my throat. My stomach flip-flopped and my head changed places with my feet. The world turned upside down.

The view changed abruptly as the blurry ground came rushing at the plane's windshield. I found my scream. I screeched as we scalped the tassels from the corn stalks. I was almost one with the corn before the plane pulled up. Then all was level except my head.

The plane soared, engines roared, and the boys shouted in glee after our plane performed a loop. Then, a strange belly-laugh surprised us all. It came from me, but it sounded like someone else. I was hysterical and it was high time to land the plane.

We were near our destination of the Sikeston, Missouri airport, a whopping four hour drive from my old Kentucky home. I laughed harder when I thought of how close I had come to a cornfield in Missouri, while out for lunch. Lucky for the pilots, I hadn't had lunch yet. The more sobering the thoughts, the more I laughed. This was my first time at hysteria.

The plane stopped on a small landing strip which resembled Owensboro's. Maybe I was having one of those dreams when you felt as if you were flying but really you just fell out of bed. I hung onto the shoulders of my flight crew of two and attempted to maneuver my Jell-O legs. The boys hoisted me into the backseat of a courtesy car which drove us to the restaurant. We entered Lamberts restaurant—"Home of the Throwed Rolls."

My stomach refused to migrate to its normal position after being thrown for a loop. A throwed roll bounced off my shoulder and rolled to the floor. I missed out on Lambert's soul food because I dreaded the ride home, unless it would be in a Rolls Royce. I watched as others enjoyed Lambert's sorghum, black-eyed peas, and chicken livers, but I couldn't even look at the corn.

I arrived alive in Kentucky and my loopy airplane experience transformed into a daring tale of adventure. To hear me tell it later, you would think I was a member of the Blue Angels. It was only too bad the whole Lambert's roll routine was lost on me because my plane took a roll first.

22

WEDDING CRASHERS

Is this the little girl I carried, Is this the little boy at play?

"If you like this, we'll sing it and throw in another song for free." My friend, Itsy, and I harmonized a verse from Sunrise, Sunset when trying-out for wedding singing gigs. We were cheap too, only requesting an open invitation to the reception. A variety of songs was not our forte, but the two we knew, we knew well: Sunrise, Sunset and The Rose. I could play two additional songs on the piano, but It's a Heartache and Three Times a Lady were hardly appropriate wedding songs.

Our old stand-by songs were taken on the road too as we sung before crowds at Windy Hollow's music hall and Goldie's Opryhouse. Goldie's used to be located where the Malco Theater was. Only the Palace in Los Angeles was older than the Malco. Someday I would tell my children that I once sang in what was the second oldest movie house in America.

That was my short claim to fame because afterwards, I was told that I did not have an authentic country music voice. While I was heartbroken, my mom exclaimed, "Thank the Lord!" She explained, "You can't be who you're not." My insufficient twang was good enough for weddings or high school musicals. I once played the lead role of Laurie in Oklahoma! It was my fault poor Jud was dead.

Mom was right; I was not a country music sensation, but I was the wedding singer. I lost count of how many basement receptions, kegs of beer, missed bouquets, and father-daughter dances I witnessed at weddings. If singing was involved, chances were I was singing in it...for free or for an empty champagne glass.

The songs never wavered, but the accompanists requested practices in unison. One night, while preparing for the next day's wedding, the guitar player offered Itsy and me a ride home. He drove us into a ditch first. In his defense, the road was like an ice rink after a Zamboni slicked it. His car slid, lop-sided into the ditch on West 5th Road until I was pinned underneath two passengers and a guitar. The driver's door became the ceiling and we became the wedding crashers. Without cell phones or ice skates, we were stuck until passing motorists and a wrecker came to our rescue. The next day, The Rose went off without a hitch and the engaged couple was happily hitched.

Itsy and I continued to sing in weddings, and still just the two songs. After college, we sang in a mutual friend's wedding. Mary was our sorority sister, but before that, a fellow high school cheerleader, and even before that, Mary was Johnny's sister, the hunk from fourth grade. Mary's groom-to-be also invited a fellow fraternity brother, Randy, to sing in the wedding along with us, after confirming that he could harmonize to Sunrise, Sunset. Our singing group got along jolly well at the reception, but when the wedding ended, the new singer skipped town.

The Wedding Singers

Two weeks later, Randy the wedding singer, called from a Texas truck stop to ask me for a date. The act of calling from a pay phone said a lot about his intentions. To step into a see-through glass booth with a dime in hand took guts. It was only one step up from sending smoke signals in order to communicate. To speak with the person you wished to call, you first had to ask the operator, who was always a woman. I pictured her being the same woman, ever-present and all encompassing. It really was up to her whether the phone call went through. A calling card was supposed to expedite long distance calls, but a series of forty numbers had to be dialed first. It was impossible to remember the sequence unless you had been drinking.

Miraculously, Randy's call got through. When he asked that I meet him across the Ohio River in Indiana, to drive to Illinois together, I accepted the date invitation, but reminded the handsome caller I was in Kentucky. I asked, "Which of those states do you live in?"

"None of them. I live in Missouri, in a little town you've never heard of called Sikeston. There's nothing there except a restaurant famous for its throwed rolls. We'll go there someday."

Oh, I had heard of it all right. After confirming that his preferred mode of transportation was a car, I agreed to the date and said, "Let's Roll."

You never really knew what life would throw you next. To make this love story short, I enjoyed the second chance of having rolls thrown at me, and learned to read lips, especially the words, "Will you marry me?" I smiled and nodded my head 'yes' along with a thumbs-up. The last time I made those gestures, my world turned upside down. My stomach felt the same lurch as I took the plunge and became engaged to be married.

While swamped with wedding plans, I expected several calls from the caterer and florist. The phone rang constantly, but one particular caller asked for Michelle. The ice cream man was not going to give up until I changed all of my names. It was his last chance to speak or forever hold his peace, but I was not about to let him talk dirty to me before my wedding. I would hear no evil, yet my ears had to be pierced somehow, and soon.

After the phone call, I sat down to the highlighted Clairol Make-up mirror and iced my ears. I held between my fingers two gifts from my husband-to-be. The pearl earring studs were beautiful, even up against the pink sponge rollers I slept in for big hair on the wedding day. I felt the earrings pierce my ears for the first time. I pierced my ears for my groom.

With studs in place, all was well on the eve of our wedding until the phone rang again. The caller claimed that some fraternal kidnappers were holding my fiancé hostage at a local golf course. Only his true love could ransom his unclothed body, tied to the tee box and covered with goop, birdseed, and Heaven knew what.

Bride and groom managed to make it to the church on time to be married at St. Stephens Cathedral on Locust Street, the place of the wedding proposal. As a child, my dad and I had passed many Saturday nights walking to St. Stephen's Mass from his office at Western

Kentucky Gas. Then, the crumpled sidewalks to the church were perfect for playing, "Step on a crack, break your mama's back," while Dad rushed me along to make it to the church on time. In 1989, I rushed to the same church in high heels on the same crumpled sidewalks, trying not to break my own back. This time Dad didn't have to pull me down the aisle.

The cathedral's buttresses still loomed overhead, but gaudy gold no longer covered the saints in glitz. The old church had had a makeover. Despite the new look, the cooling system was still the old one, and wedding guests did not notice the fresh decor in the August heat when the air conditioner blew a fuse.

My groom had sweat beads pouring from his face. I had tears pouring from mine. If we could make it through the ceremony without melting, the marriage would be a piece of cake. Our own wedding called for a new song, so we rushed through a song dedicated to our parents, Wind Beneath my Wings. We were both wedding singers and what better way to begin a marriage? Singing and in heat. The heatwave caused the wedding homily to be shortened, but not short enough to prevent the tainting of my husband's pet nickname for me.

My toddler brother, Van, was the wedding ring bearer. He naturally mispronounced words like elephant and porcupine. Randy called me "Piney," short for 'corkypine,' a.k.a. porcupine. It was silly but cute until the priest mutilated it when reading our personal love letters aloud during the ceremony. In his private letter, Randy called me "Piney," which the priest mispronounced "Peeny." Finally, Father Bradley ended the love letter with "My little Peeny."

Wedding guests murmured, "What did he call her?"

and "Did he call her what I think he called her?" The moment was ruined as was the nickname. By then, all my names had been changed, and with good reason.

After the ceremony, husband and wife did not make it to the reception before all the food was devoured. Five hundred of our friends and family attended the party at the Cigar Factory Mall atrium, which was once a seven story tobacco warehouse. In 1892, the Cigar Factory was the largest wooden building in the world. In 1989, five hundred guests went through five kegs of beer in the same building. Our wedding night was spent at the Executive Inn, but the buffet was closed by the time we arrived. I was so hungry I would have eaten the frog legs.

But I was happy to be happily married. My heart sang while my ears rang. On our honeymoon night, I discovered the reason for the ringing. A piece of birdseed had lodged in my left ear when well-wishers threw it at the happy couple before we left in our 'Just

Married' car. Not only would I hear no evil, I would not hear anything unless the bird food was removed.

After twenty-five years of marriage, I can still hear. Time really did fly, like the little plane which flew me over my future home on Kate Drive in Sikeston, Missouri, right down the road from the Home of the Throwed Rolls. I have thoroughly enjoyed this wild ride, loops and all.

23

AND THAT'S THE WAY IT WAS

"Some say love it is a river..." Remnants of The Rose song lyrics drifted through my mind as my eyes tracked a piece of driftwood that dodged barges on the river's obstacle course. The double-wide barges pushed by tiny tugboats reminded me of Little Toot, the tugboat afraid to tug. Staring at them was like watching life float past in an old-fashioned diorama of Row, row, row your boat. If you twisted the knob faster, the backdrop furiously flashed scenes until coming back to the beginning. Such was life in the Big O, coming full circle as the new day dawned.

It is 2014 and the bridge is open again after a new blue paint job. I witnessed the sun rise above the bridge just as the barge passed underneath it. A black stray cat scurried inside the ornamental grass. I chuckled and thought of the legendary black cat which prowled Downtown Owensboro at night to search for souls to steal for the devil. This little kitty was merely searching for scraps and licking dried ketchup from the patio.

When I walked out the door this morning, the summer heat hit me in the face. It was going to be another day where you could smell the asphalt melting. I was reminded of my teenhood where I spent hot days like this at the Paddock Swim Club. The coconut scent, bronzed bodies, and burnt orange color of Sun-in couldn't be copied, but as I stood up from the river's metal swing, I had the same kind of marks that I used to get on the backs of my summer thighs from the pool lawn chairs.

In the middle of my present heatwave, I visualized a frozen Ohio River as it was in 1918. The temperature was -16 degrees when Owensboro citizens crossed the river to Indiana while walking on water. The river had frozen over again since then, but barges now broke the ice before people had a chance to break their necks. In 1976, monolithic columns of ice and snow lined the riverbanks, only leaving a skinny waterway wide enough for one barge at a time. If walkers wanted to chance the icy river, they would have to climb a Mount Kilimanjaro peak first.

Some winters, the river did not recognize its boundaries. In January of 1937, the river crested at almost 55 feet. The flooded river covered 90,959 of Daviess County's 282,545 acres, making Owensboro akin to Atlantis. Even with sweat beads trickling down my back, I shivered when thinking of our town as a muddy-toned swamp.

So much had changed in my hometown, yet some things never would. Our roots reached deep down, as far as the river was deep. While outward appearances varied, the apple still didn't fall far from the tree-not that the Big

O was anything like the Big Apple. Even so, I was surprised at Owensboro's multi-cultural flavor when I last revisited it. When I strolled along the River Walk, while keeping to the right to allow joggers and dogs on leashes to pass, I heard sprinklings of Spanish. One mother and son paused to ask me the name of the river in front of them. Two more teenagers offered me a piece of pizza from the concession stand. I would have accepted if I hadn't just eaten an entire mashed potato pizza from the gourmet pizza parlor next door.

A hippy-themed trailer was parked in the lot across the street while the American Legion's flags waved wildly in the wind. Cars honked as hollering kids weaved in and out of tunnels and a bass fish's mouth while their canopied strollers remained vacant under the concrete trees. Young couples shared porch swings overlooking the river and café tables were chock-full of folks gobbling up the free Wi-Fi as they guzzled beer and policemen patrolled past. The bright sun ricocheted from the silver chrome of the swings and benches while the blue bridge appeared as silver and reflected over the river. The view was breathtaking.

The river scene teemed with life. Beauty ambushed you at every turn with fountains playing along with strumming banjos. The music was constant, and statues acted as if even they were listening for the beat. When the live bands ceased and the fountains rested momentarily, one could hear a faint plunking of Bluegrass music piped in from somewhere. One fountain sprayed its guests as they sat on the edge. There was always that one particular seat where you would get soaked, just like at Sea World.

Owensboro's river makeover featured a massive waterfall cascading over steps where the boat launch used to be. The old ramp was a sideways parking lot which threatened to tumble the leaning cars and boats into the river. With the waterfall taking the place of the levee, only chlorinated water slid down the steep banks now. The stone terrace served an aesthetic purpose with a glass splintering screech alerting unsuspecting visitors to the water avalanche which followed and sometimes spilled into the river.

Just past the waterfall, a shell of many colors mingled with the approaching pink sunset. People lined the rails to view the sun dropping like the Times Square ball. Instantly, the sky was bathed in crimson, with the river turning red as the sun slipped into it. Some clapped as if at a sorority chapter meeting, or maybe from the massive margaritas from the patio bar.

I stared over the railing at the moving current. I once was leery of stepping foot in river after seeing the wooly mammoth fossils at the area museum. The beasts' bones were supposedly found at the bottom of this river. I could not help but think of their hairy bodies and pointed tusks while just dipping my toes in the water from the side of a boat. The river used to be a popular place for folks to be baptized. Believers formed lines to be dunked in the river water and weren't afraid of what lurked under the waves. I would have liked to have witnessed those, the baptisms, that is.

For a moment I forgot where I was until the tobacco scent cantered across the breeze and the water foamed below with speed boats hanging out under the bridge, now with their low beam lights reflecting. It was still the same old Owensboro. Instead of an Army brat, I was a river brat. Take me to the river just don't drop me in the water, especially off the bridge. I enjoyed my passing time here but was used to having it all to myself. I would have to get used to the eclectic crowd.

For at least ten years, a sign leading into town read: City of Owensboro Population 52,000. After a decade, the 2 on the sign was replaced with a 4. For another twenty years, the city population held firm at 54,000. Owensboro was slow to change but was always on the move, just like the river. The current population is now a steady 58,400.

I would not go as far as to say that Owensboro welcomed change, but it did welcome its visitors. Unlike other small towns, it did not lure visitors away from their money and then hope they would leave soon; we wanted visitors to stay and to return.

Just as the water from the new waterfall flowed, a visitor could visibly relax once he immersed himself in the timed intervals and rhythm of the great gushes. Everything was safe and planned. That was the Owensboro I grew up with. My river of memories continued as I reminisced further on the car ride with my mom and daughter to visit a relative's gravesite.

The serene backdrop of Brown's Valley reminded me of King David's Psalm 23: Even though I walk through the darkest valley, I will fear no evil. Like a Currier & Ives setting, our drive led to a verdant pasture surrounding a charming country church. He makes me lie down in green pastures…He refreshes my soul. (NIV) I had roamed the church grounds and cemetery since I was a little girl visiting relatives' graves. There were just more rows of them now. I had listened to the tales behind the tombstones, from the one about an uncle with an artificial leg to the one about my great grandmother blessing believers financially from beyond the grave.

After the 2000 tornado demolished Aunt Mary's farm, a wooden leg was found among the debris. Since the artificial leg story was found to be true, the money one might be too. If it wasn't, it ought to be. I remembered the steep cemetery hill where I tried to keep from running down in order to help Memaw pick the asparagus that grew at the bottom of the graveled drive. We never ate the asparagus while at the cemetery because of unspoken cemetery rules. Everyone knew you weren't supposed to eat and run at a cemetery. Much had changed since then, but the rules, never. Now my Memaw was laid to rest and the asparagus grew no more. On the way back to town, we drove past a field of tobacco. When I grew up, we didn't use tobacco for anything but chewing or smoking. I tried both and failed at both. I once opened a can of snuff to inhale, but it blew into my eyes instead. Not good. I also tried to blow smoke rings while at various field parties held in the actual fields the tobacco-filled cigarettes came from. That was when I found out about my tobacco allergy.

Owensboro's tobacco crop looked good from where I sat in the passenger seat. Perhaps tobacco farmers would make a comeback with the crop in recent news. Owensboro's tobacco was being used in the making of cat vaccinations and Ebola shots. That was good news for us cat owners, but even better for a worldwide pandemic. When one of the first Americans contracted the deadly Ebola virus, a special tobacco concoction was rushed to Atlanta's Emory Hospital for the patient. It would be a twist of fate for Kentucky farmers to be compensated by the government to grow more tobacco. But there would always be some diehard chain smoker who got the wrong idea. "You mean I can inject tobacco in me?" (Kentucky.com)

We now passed a cornfield I recognized. Since Mom was driving, I lifted my cell phone discreetly to take a picture and did not want to draw attention to what I was doing. I intended to text a private picture to my husband in Alabama to see if he recognized the cornfield where we used to make out.

Before the cornfield was completely out of range, my mother looked in the rear-view mirror and said to my daughter, "Your Pop and I used to go parking in that cornfield."

"Wow!" I blurted out. "We did too."

My mom continued, "One time we got stuck and had to call Uncle Joe to get us unstuck. My biggest fear was that my brothers would find out what I was doing."

"Wow," I said again. "I was afraid of farmers shooting at us, but my biggest fear was that you and Dad would find out where I was."

"This is just so wrong," my daughter said from the back seat as she clasped her hands over her ears and eyes while I snapped a picture of the passing corn. It was actually so right. Life mostly stayed the same. Of all things, the corn did not change. Who knew these fields were steeped in family tradition? My daughter would understand soon and change her tune. Within weeks, she would become engaged to a Southern beau from Alabama. Thank heavens Alabama cotton didn't grow as tall as Kentucky corn.

24

YOU MIGHT BE FROM OWENSBORO IF...

You know that burgoo rhymes with thank you, not bird doo.

You know the correct pronunciation of Louisville is "Lulvul."

You think you can drive a race car.

You know the Big Dipper is much more than a constellation.
You know what the "Big O" is and what the "Big E" was.
A bad cough is best treated with whiskey.
A fur piece means a long ways down the road.
A strip pit is something you swim in after you strip.
You enjoy Moonlite in the daylight even without Starlite.
Frog legs taste like chicken to you.
You can ride the Windy Hollow bull on any given Sunday.
You set the tobacco and top it before smoking it.
You know that double dribbling has nothing to do with slobbering a lot.
You like your hamburger through the garden.
You thank God it's Friday after five.
Waiting means holding off until the corn is tall enough to hide your car.
PCB is the place you spend KEA.
It makes sense that Christian County is wet but Bourbon County is dry.
You can go from Kentucky to Indiana in five minutes via the Ohio River.
Your All-American City happens to be the world's barbeque capital.

Happy bicentennial, Owensboro!

ABOUT THE AUTHOR

Shelly Van Meter Miller was born in Owensboro, KY. She graduated from Murray State University with a Bachelor of Science in Speech Communication. After college, she worked as a press aide for a United States Senator in Washington, D.C. before marrying her husband and settling in Madison, Alabama. Together, she and her husband raised three girls in the South.

Shelly is the Indie Award Winning Author of *Tornado Valley: Huntsville's Havoc* and author of *Whispered Secrets of the South: Montevallo, Alabama,* first volume in a new book series. *Whispered Secrets* was featured as historical fiction book of the day by Freebooksy. Visit her fan page at www.writebabywrite.org.

She taught aerobics and pregnancy exercise classes throughout the community and even completed a half-marathon. Yes, you read it correctly, "half." She considers that to be good enough. She then homeschooled her children and exercised her writing muscle by grading stacks of research papers. She was fired from that job when her children went to public school.

Nowadays, Shelly finds her muse in the garden. She became a Master Gardener to have an excuse to work at what she loves. Her ideal day is spent writing in the garden. Careful, because if you ask her what she does all day, she will say "nothing," unless she is chasing her three cats.

OTHER BOOKS BY THIS INDIE AWARD WINNING AUTHOR

Tornado Valley: Huntsville's Havoc

Touchdown! Folks in Alabama don't know whether to cheer or run when hearing the expression. Touchdown could mean that we've just won another football National Championship or it could indicate that a tornado is on the ground. I could never be a storm chaser. I'm the one the storm chases. Funnels circle around me like shark fins as I bow my head in a school hallway, kneel down in a convent, or give birth to a newborn baby wailing in unison with the tornado sirens. I huddle with toddlers in showers and beg for shelter in a McDonald's freezer. I remain a sitting duck in a second-floor apartment, and find myself in the wrong place at the wrong time while in the emergency room with storm victims.

Life in the Rocket City is a thrill ride which is not for the faint of heart, this I know. So brace yourself for a front row seat on a ride through Tornado Valley! Alabama is the home of the world's deadliest twisters, and Huntsville is in the heart of the arena. Our space history is out of this world, but our tornado history will blow you away.

Take a rollercoaster ride through the history of Alabama tornadoes before plunging into the gripping story of the Day of Devastation. Witness the stars falling on Alabama in 1833. Then get ready for the sky to fall! The plot twists as Huntsville's torrid tornado past comes alive in the 1974 Super Tornado Outbreak. The rollercoaster corkscrews as it encounters an unexpected twister in 1989 that slingshots the reader into the angry vortex on Airport Road.

The ride cruises before taking another gut-wrenching dive that catapults its riders into an inverted twist from yet another Anderson Hills tornado in 1995. The town turns upside-down but Huntsville survives, revives, and thrives. But the worst is yet to come. Another tornado season is just around the corner. Beware of the month of April, especially on a Wednesday.

The warning sirens wail, we're bombarded by softball-sized hail, and an EF3 tornado slams into the jail. It's just another day in Alabama, but the countdown clock is ticking. The next tornado warning could be "the one." Our voice drops to a whisper when we mention an EF5. We realize life is too short. The coaster accelerates. Can you feel the torque? We have no idea what's around the next bend.

Suddenly, the nightmare comes true as the ride zooms out of control, this time in a free-fall on April 27, 2011. Alabama is bombarded by a record 62 tornadoes in one day. Abruptly, the ride comes to a screeching halt. The adrenaline rush subsides. You've just experienced Huntsville's Havoc. Immediately the passengers ask one another, "Do you want to ride again?" Some will and some swear, never again.

Available at http://www.writebabywrite.org

Whispered Secrets of the South: Montevallo AL

Lions, and crooks, and ghosts, oh my! Far from an exotic movie set location, Montevallo is a quaint college town in the heart of Alabama. You won't believe the stories from its rural past. Of course, you shouldn't believe everything you hear anyway. Some tales are charming, some surreal, and others border on the absurd. Still, you wonder…no one could make this stuff up.

Jean Michelle's daughter is a student at the University of Montevallo. During parent visits, Jean Michelle stumbles upon a gateway into the past on the University of Montevallo's campus. She travels through time to discover if the rumors are true. Only, the characters of the past believe she's Sally, someone they already know. She journeys through Cherokee Indian territory with the infamous Red Eagle and sneaks a glimpse of Reynolds Hall's makeshift Civil War hospital.

A wedding feast turns into a disaster at the King Mansion when an uninvited ghost cuts in during a dance. But this may be Jean Michelle's only chance to investigate where Mr. King buried his treasure from the Yankees. Jean Michelle experiences College Night firsthand and must choose a side. The nation's oldest homecoming tradition is directed behind the scenes by a ghost who likes surprises. Will it be a PV or a GV3?

She even knocks on Condie's door and meets the former Alabama College's most famous resident. No one can forget the girl on fire, especially her face. Jean Michelle returns to the beautiful campus quad where she started her quest. But the familiar Eclipse cat winks as if something is amiss. She has seen that cat somewhere before. Imagine her surprise when the past catches up with her. Numerous sightings of the historical characters are spotted in the present at Montevallo's American Village. The only legend missing in action is Sasquatch, although he was recently spotted in nearby Chilton County.

History literally comes alive on the University of Montevallo's campus. Ghosts of the past linger and appear when least expected. Perhaps there's more to this geographical center of Alabama than just purple spirit or golden pride. Should Jean Michelle reveal the secrets whispered to her from the past? Two can keep a secret if one of them is dead. Benjamin Franklin first spoke these wise words, but he is dead. Which reminds me, Montevallo should be added to your list of places to see before you die.

Montevallo, Alabama's Whispered Secrets of the South is the first in a series of books which unravel the untold secrets of small Southern towns. From church bells, train rails, calaboose jails to ghost tales, this book reeks of wisteria, sweet tea, hospitality, and swinging porch doors. Although the stories are fictional, they are riddled with real-life histories and mysteries. You can decide which is which.

Note: The cat's name has been changed to protect his identity.

Available at http://www.writebabywrite.org

Write, Baby, Write: You Can Do It!

So you want to be a writer? Over eighty percent of people surveyed believe they have a book in them, yet few pursue their writing dreams. While time and talent are essential, writing and finishing a book is more than just sitting down to the daily grind.

Writer's candy dangles from paragraph to paragraph and is ripe for the picking in Write, Baby, Write. Sample delights include muse and creativity, finding your voice, keeping a word bank, the best time to write, story starters and other goodies only writers get excited about. Use the fresh strategies for your own novel-in-the-making as you glean inspiration from the greats. Famous quotes from outstanding authors are interspersed for motivation.

Are you ready to complete your writing masterpiece? There were times I honestly didn't think I had it in me. At other times, nothing could stop me from writing. In Write, Baby, Write, I leave it all on the field. Fellow writers are invited along on my personal journey as we plug through the hard stuff in order to bask in the writing bliss sure to come. You, too, will discover many "Aha!" moments of assurance that you are on the right track.

This book is tailored to encourage both the beginning writer who needs a gentle push to start, and the seasoned writer suffering from a comparison syndrome. Writing and finishing a book which will outlive you can be one of life's most fulfilling accomplishments. Now is the time to put the finishing touches on your work of art and see your writing dreams come true. For all writers and wanna-be writers, this book is for you!

Available at http://www.writebabywrite.org

MY BIG O JOURNEY

Made in the USA
San Bernardino, CA
05 December 2018